As the Shadows Play Around Us

As the Shadows Play Around Us

A Collection of Stories, Poetry and Essays

Warren Sunkar

***

Copyright © 2016 Warren Sunkar

The moral right of the author has been asserted.

All rights reserved.

No part of this publication may be reproduced, stored in a retrieval system, or transmitted, in any form or by any means, without the prior permission in writing of the publisher, nor be otherwise circulated in any form of binding or cover other than that in which it is published and without a similar condition including this condition being imposed on the subsequent purchaser.

National Library of Australia Cataloguing-in-Publication entry

Creator: Sunkar, Warren, author.

Title: As the shadows play around us / Warren Sunkar.

ISBN: 9780995371606 (paperback)

Subjects: Short stories. Poetry. Essays.

Dewey Number: A820.8

Publishing Consultants: Pickawoowoo Publishing Group

(interior & cover layout)

Thank you

Our Divine Father and Mother

With A Special Dedication to:

Sadiki Bakari,

Whose Great Light is being seen, here,

on the other side of the world.

Foreword

Divine Love is not a quality of the personality. It is free from all taints and disturbances. Divine love manifests only when one is self-surrendered in the eternal moment of God. It is Christ incarnated, Grace given from that which lies beyond all grasping and conception.

People confuse such blessing with the feeling states that such touches bring them. They then seek to grasp the unattainable rather than just let go and allow the ever new moment of Love to reveal itself again and again...

Warren Sunkar

Contents

As the Shadows Play Around Us	iii
Foreword	vi
CREATIVE WORKS	1
The Call	2
In Chorus With Wolves	4
What Manner Of Love Is This?	7
Ayahuasca Dreaming	9
Tears Upon The Battlefield	19
Such A Strange Thing	24
The Selfless Flower	26
Chops	30
Gaia Laments	40
Through the Veil	43
The Dawn Lovers	47
So Does A Lie Meet Its End	50

The Graveyard Vagabond	55
Unutterable Love	57
The Heart That Searches	59
The Ark of Christ	62
ESOTERIC ARTICLES	67
Open The Window Of Grace	68
Fall On Your Feet…Not On Your Head!	73
False Offerings	79
Into the Dark Night	84
The God of Illusions	89
Darkness is Rising	99
The Beast	105
Beware of Feeding Drama	110
For Those Intrepid Warriors Of Love	115
The Fire of God's Love	120
A Child of Universal Love	123

CREATIVE WORKS

The Call

I must leave for I hear the song of destiny and know that she sings for me. Her gentle voice, more alluring than a siren's serenade, takes my soul and caresses my broken heart, drawing out such longing that it runs down my cheeks as tears when I am alone.

She speaks to me in my dreams and asks me to leave behind all selfishness and to throw off all learning for it is misconception and to go and stand naked in the sun.

Embarrassed, I hide but she understands I am timid and lifts me out of my darkness with the warmth of her smile. She tells me not to be ashamed of my nakedness for the vanity and pride that man clothes himself in is sickness and such a mask hides his inner smile.

She asks me to let go of yesterday for she dances not there, to be in the now for it holds no expectations and that the past I hold myself to, therein contains my suffering.

Yet I fear, for uncertainty takes me as I think about loss and worry about failure, but as I look out to the horizon of love stretched out before me I find my strength in the realisation that there isn't any.

I must walk alone for the way to her heart is a path that only I can see.

Alone, sometimes the thought scares me but then I look into the eyes of my loved ones around me and I find them weeping. Then I realise that already we are alone and that I am hiding amongst them and them with me.

Then upon the comforting wings of inspiration my Destiny whispers; "Beloved, though you may walk amongst a thousand loving and familiar faces, always will your heart yearn for me.

"My call is the summons to Truth, my kiss is the silence of all your desires, I am your completion in death and your birth to infinity.

"Side by side, we will find comfort in each other for I will stand by you when the loving is lost and the thousand familiar faces turn away.

"Hand in hand, together, we will walk into the unknown…"

I must leave for I hear the song of destiny and know that she sings for me. She is a daughter of beauty, a goddess who beckons me to give chase through fields of eternity in hope that I might catch and embrace her in fiery love, where together we will shine as a single star and watch the dawn of a New World open before us…

IN CHORUS WITH WOLVES

We stood overlooking a city. In the distance, the streaming and flickering lights of neon and traffic thriving upon a circuit board of streets lit up the night sky before us through a dull smoky haze. The strange and mixed sounds of civilization, ever constant, ever present, echoed to our ears from below. Holding one another, we looked out into the vastness of space as the sun disappeared beyond sight and shadow spread across the world.

Babylon had risen before us...

As timid children we stand before this darkness with fluttering hearts, breathless and vulnerable as the wails of earth reach fever pitch. Wayward humanity chained to its dying world. Hiding behind its fear and ignorance in a futile attempt to escape from that which must come to pass – do we stand today over a global civilization that shall now collapse fast upon itself.

My friend took my hand firmly and I welcomed her.

"Has it come to this?" she whispered, as a tear ran down her cheek, her eyes reflected my own heart's sorrow.

"What does come, must be," I whispered to her ear.

"This wayward world does defy its soul and the dark night of these times settles upon us. This world's lost children in their defiance and arrogance now turn upon themselves in their futility and desperation. Humanity has denied its true birthright."

Her body shuddered as the great travesty of human life opened in the great drama unfolding before us.

She wept openly. "Forgotten is the song of Love upon this earth. A growing madness possesses the world, the darkened gods of man are failing and their keepers cry for blood. The rulers seek to throw such a chain around this world that they may break humanity's back. Loud is the cry of arrogance and falsehood; wolves circle and the shadows of fear taunt and dance around us.

"Would we dare weather this storm when it is all so hopeless?"

I answered: "Today, upon this fallen earth we walk within the growing madness and tensions of these times. Do not succumb to those waves of fear and despair that can temporarily engulf us. In these days of darkness and confusion let us find our repose in the silence of our hearts and forget not our heritage as children of God. We are called to stay true to our deepest heart's calling."

Her eyes glittered in the moonlight.

I whispered: "The veil of earth often seems so impenetrable and thick, yet these images that parade before us are not real. Do not identify with this transient reality. Though Love may seem to hide its face in such times it is ever present for those whose hearts are faithful and pure.

"These are the days warned by the prophets and seers of humanity's past. And in this darkest hour we are those who are called to stand amidst this almighty tempest.

"We are guided by the great truths sung upon the lips of those avatars that have walked this fallen earth for us. And remember, though the passing storm may eclipse the light it cannot vanquish the sun."

Her hands tightened in mine. "I need to remember!"

"Then still yourself and surrender unto the will of the Father. Let the cares of the world fall away for in truth they have no substance."

Her eyes looked deep into mine searching their depths and then together we looked up. In the timelessness of a sigh we let go as the living torch of love between us flared. The clouds of confusion and obscurity were dissolved and the light of Love divine glowed around us and a wave of ecstasy rippled and pulsed through us.

She cried out in tears of joy: "I remember!"

With the blessing of angels, in the darkest of nights, looking out over the city did we dare sing Love's song upon this fallen earth. Carried upon the winds did it find its way into the hearts of those who were open.

The earth tremored under our feet, as lightning rippled around us.

The rulers faltered, the wolves whimpered, and in their howls of fear joined us in chorus…

Our hearts gave praise.

What Manner Of Love Is This?

You asked what manner of love is this?
That has estranged us from this world,
Where the laughter of human voices
Are but wails of pain and torment
Where loneliness is one's closest friend.
We walk the path
And we struggle as the mud of the world
Clings to our feet,
Yet the call of Christ harkens our pace
And mostly we are blind
For the way is not seen with our eyes
But felt within our hearts,
And the dark ones laugh and whisper to us
"Fools, turn back, you shall become as dust"
But dust we know we already are
And turn back we shall not
For the thread of true life we hold.
Unto its guidance we surrender

Warren Sunkar

And naught can dampen our hearts resolve
For this world means nothing to us
And for this love we walk the razor's edge
Towards new life that beckons us
And upon this way we shall perish
Yet arise in glory and flame,
And when this earthly task is done
We shall disappear into the great
silence of the dark
The light of which man knows not
The eternal spirit from whence we came.

Ayahuasca Dreaming

It was just after sunset and we sat upon the floor.

As I poured the brown liquid I briefly pondered the unexpected synchronicities that had brought us together for such an event. A tingling sensation went through my body and I was aware that the plant was speaking to me. I smiled, we had heard the stories of others and now it was time for an experience of our own.

It was said that the Teacher Plant had a consciousness that would communicate with those who received it with an open mind and heart.

In an unspoken trust we shared a couple of bowls of the brew between us not knowing what to expect and the four of us drank down the bitter potion with distaste.

As the bowls were drained, we lay upon our backs surrendering to a metaphysical journey into the unknown…

Staring at the ceiling, slow, conscious minutes ticked by…

Nestling into the thin mattress underneath me, my sense of self began to gently dissipate into a soft ethereal glow that gently infused me with splashes of warmth that washed through my body.

Rising, dissolving, expanding into greater freedom, my diminishing consciousness of time slowly began dissolving in vapours of love as my awareness of five-sense reality began melting like butter upon a stovetop.

Relaxing, we lightened to become unexpectedly aware of a spritely spirit of earth. Feminine and playful, she darted and hovered between us in a loving and flirtatious dance. Playing with us in a sensual and unabashed manner she caressed all those who were in the room. Diving through the air, she washed herself through me, kissing me on my lips as I laughed in delighted surprise.

I could feel her healing ethereal touches all over my body as her voice whispered beautiful imagery into my mind as my body shivered in blissful response.

I laughed out aloud as she poked my stomach in a soft jest to let me know she could condense and materialise.

As she played, two other kinds of earthen spirits were unveiled and lovingly nestled into my side. I lay on my back stroking them gently as they nuzzled me in a sweet affection.

As I lay there, I could hear and feel my friends around me. Each one was sharing such an experience as the spritely earth spirit swam around the room blessing each of them with her delicious aura that bathed those she touched in kisses of bliss as she whispered visions and voices of love and affirmation.

Shutting my eyes, resting deeper into the experience, the veil of the unseen dissolved before me. We could understand that the Ayahausca plant was a living key and energetic link to that which was the spirit of the earth.

Suddenly, I could feel the ethers above us deeply stir as a dimensional portal opened.

A quickening pulse took me from within and I felt the presence of the Great Guardian.

I looked up as this ultra-terrestrial of light opened the gateway above me to touch my aura with its rainbow of colours and energies.

Unlocking within a deep remembrance, I felt a strong kinship and affiliation with this great multi-dimensional intelligence and I gasped in splendour as this benevolent insectoid drew back the dimensional veils between us and the vibrations of light quickened through the room to engulf us all.

Shutting my eyes, I was raised into an exploding fractal vision of shimmering colours and cascading rivers of pulsing living energies. Waves of ecstasy washed through my body as I launched into the pool of lights around me.

A chameleon of changing vibrations, I shifted gently yet swiftly through the thin veils of dimension. Twirling and spinning in a dance of joy with the ease and grace enlivened from a remembrance, experienced beyond the confines of body consciousness.

Suddenly, I found myself standing in a jungle clearing.

Bright psychic light shimmered all around as exotic birds and insects in symphony adorned the spectacular vision of the world I stood within.

Before me stood four shamans. They were ancient ones, powerful and impressive as they bowed solemnly. Awe inspiring in their headdress of colourful plumage, I bowed in the presence of these teachers. Then in silence we sat in a circle and communed with closed eyes.

I began to fall backwards and upwards into the vast expanse of space as images flashed rapidly through my mind's eye in a collage of information.

I received a forgotten history of secret and dark things. All hidden today behind a movie version of reality, within which we are manipulated and maintained by the nefarious keepers of our world. I cried out in horror as alien beings looked upon humanity with cold, predatory eyes.

A profound sadness took my heart as before me opened a storyboard of tragedy. Holding me in an embrace of love, the teacher plant guided me to a deeper understanding of the mostly unseen happenings here upon this earth.

Humanity's sad history entwined with these Greys.

These lost and foreign beings had altered the human race by genetically tampering, implanting and controlling them. Humanity has been not unlike lab rats to these foreign beings and I reeled before the sickening vision of what has happened in humanity's past and what goes on still today from the shadows.

The visions and teachings came with an increasing rapidity which downloaded through my awareness as the Teacher Plant communicated, helping me to understand and remember. I opened further into the experience, trusting the guidance to see the truth of the planetary situation.

The anguish of humanity took my heart as I was expanded to see how humanity was being kept from its true potentiality. How we are all being manipulated into a vibratory prison with most of the populace unknowing of their fate.

Upon this earth, all are subject to occult enslavement and are energetically paralysed by those beings that exist outside the now extremely limited bandwidth of humanity's vibratory perception.

I shuddered as I saw within the dark subterranean levels of the planet reptilians hissing from the shadows.

Falling backwards I became aware once again of the presence of my friends.

The greater light pervading the room and us all from within, dissolved any sense of separation as we had all melded as one in psychic unity.

We were as open books to one another and nothing was kept hidden as we accessed each other's thought streams and life waves. Hidden secrets, joys, and fears were shared between us as visual transmissions as the night went on slipping in and out of a timeless blur.

As each of our lives unravelled before one another, they were played out almost cinematically. It enabled us to observe each other's burdens, weaknesses and lives without judgement or condemnation as we all saw from the greater perspective.

We rejoiced in the experience for there were only smiles in such a union as the teacher plant guided us all through the moment with a loving embrace.

I became aware of my partner lying upon a couch behind me, beginning to stir, as the teacher plant revealed to her that which she found difficult to accept.

Following her energy stream, I opened to her, sharing a vision of great tribulations coming to the planet. She witnessed humanity losing itself to madness and savagery, opening itself to planetary destruction.

She was openly weeping and shaking her head at such a possibility. I was inwardly motioned to go to her. I knelt next to the couch and gently put my arms around her as she burrowed into my chest. Holding her, comforting her, I ran my hands through her hair as she curled foetally, tears running down her cheeks.

As I shut my eyes again a pre-earth remembrance awoke from within both of us.

As stars we flew through space beyond the heavy and suffocating clouds and confines of earth's density, playing as children of Love. We saw our life threads circling and entwining in a dance of joy and innocence as we felt our connection run much deeper than the short relationship that we share in our earthly personalities.

Then we saw others of our greater family, stars of light, responding to the cry of Gaia and her humanity as we answered in a wave of Love to descend and penetrate into the darkened sphere of earth, to seed this planet for its birth into its cosmic initiation.

The night sped on as we all throbbed in ecstasy, plunged into a vortex of imagery and unutterable revelation, unfiltered by the limitations of mind.

Each message personal yet shared, as each of us taking that which was meant for them. The playful spirit darting and dancing between us all, giving healings and comfort as each of us gasped or laughed at the revelations and messages given them.

Then softly, in an inner dawning of soul stirring and arousing, not unlike a soft crescendo of a playing violin, a haunting song arose within the inner silence and its deep sadness began to take my heart as everything faded into darkness.

Majestic Gaia, like a whale of the ocean depths, was singing her lament through deep space. I was flooded with the deepest of sorrow as her call brought tears streaming down my cheeks. A deep longing rose to my lips as I moaned out aloud in deepest soul pain. Humanity had forgotten their great mother and she was calling out in her great pain and distress.

As I looked out over Earth in cosmic vision from space, I knew we were failing her. Great helplessness and shame stirred from within as the acceptance of being part of the collective that was killing her washed through me.

Overwhelmed, I cried and sang back to her through the vast expanse of space.

I was sobbing.

I looked back upon a wayward humanity, out of cosmic rhythm, crippled and poisoned. I cried out to them through space but they were so immersed in themselves that they could not hear.

Humanity, if you would only open and see, you would recoil in horror and shame at the madness you have unleashed. Your loving Mother is in such pain, open your hearts to her for she is part of you and you of her. You have forgotten her sacrifice and how she has laboured for you.

She calls for her children's love and understanding.

As I was launched again through space, a portal opened and in a surge of light and colour I was transported in a neon blur as the great cosmic womb opened before me.

Unable to resist, I merged inside.

Wave upon wave of delightful, mystical energy rippled sensually through me.

I was a solar seed to fertilise and dissolve in liquid ecstasy as my whole body throbbed in deep rhythmical orgasm.

Energy pulsed through me as a cascading shower that launched through the fountainhead of my crown in unspeakable climax, sparking within and all around me a beautiful fusion in a glorious explosion of light; a conception took place.

Crowned in mystical euphoria, a bright rainbow of light shone through me as the guardian further opened my awareness.

With spurts of energy that flooded through me I was encoded with symbols of living energy like a sun shower of rain.

A living language of glyphs and geometrical shapes awakening aspects of my being to things unknowable to the lower mind.

Slowly, the pulsing began to softly ease as my aura convulsed in joy and fulfilment.

I then began to feel the energy gently leave.

The guardian and its children slowly withdrew through their dimensional vortex and the consciousness of the Teacher Plant slowly faded from my mind's eye as the realisation of time slowly began to once again infiltrate our awareness.

Our awareness of space grew as we slowly adjusted and settled back to earthly consciousness.

Laying there, glowing, I had cuddled deep into my blanket letting go with a deep, peaceful sigh. Turning around to see smiles beaming from my friends who all just laughed aloud at the experience.

That morning, we all walked outside renewed in life as the dawning light in a halo of soft pastels christened the horizon before us. The birds in beautiful symphony made music that delighted and raised our hearts as we all greeted the coming day.

Our heightened awareness of the life glowing through us had given us a deeper communion with our Great Mother. Our vibration had been raised as such that I beheld a resonance with Gaia unknown in this short sojourn upon this earth, now understanding her great potentiality.

With a heartfelt release I thanked the Teacher Plant as I whispered to the horizon…

And I thought…

Humanity, if you would only open your little minds and hearts to embrace your own as children of Life, you would understand. You could enjoy as do birds in their morning celebration, bathing in the light of the spiritual sun.

Tears Upon The Battlefield

A young friend sat alone on the grass in the central city park unnoticed by those who were too busy. Writing poetry that surpassed her age she was a defiant heart crying in the shadows of our so-called civilization.

Struggling inwardly and bravely, her poetry whispered to me like a beautiful song that both kissed and saddened my heart.

Smiling as I approached, Madison dropped her pen and notepad in her bag and stood up to give me a warm hug. Taking her hand with a smile I guided her through those quieter and unpopulated streets and pathways. As we navigated our way through the city, we talked and laughed and the throb and blur of our surroundings went unnoticed.

Coming to a footbridge she skipped on ahead and ran up the stairs.

Sometimes we would come here to talk and reflect. A true reality check in a world gone mad and we were blessed in a simple friendship by its living flame as we struggled within the limitations of our earthly sojourn.

We walked out to the centre of the bridge, the city stood before us and its traffic moved beneath. Together, we stared out over the urban sprawl...

"Sometimes I get so scared," she broke the silence between us.

"This civilization has lost all sense and the people go about their mundane lives in a way that no longer has any true meaning. Our society seems void of purpose, everything is confused and often wrong."

She looked up at me questioningly. "It seems so overwhelming."

As I stood beside her, I could feel her deep concern and troubles.

"When humanity denies truth they lose their alignment and connection to Life. The wheel turns, a new cycle begins, all that we have invested in disappears, all that we have created turns around and bears down upon us.

"Should we seek to cling to the familiar and the comfortable now we find they are disappearing. The world as we know it is coming to its end," I answered her.

Bitterly she whispered: "This world is insane. Every day our teachers, media and peers sell us lies as truth, conformity as individuality, prison as freedom.

"My heart tells me that humanity has lost its way because they call this life," she pointed out to the horizon, "when all it is, is walking death.

"My friends succumb to this fog having lost all sense of who they truly are. Their hearts are dying and their minds corrupted by the propaganda of a decaying world order that seeks to keep them confused, sickened and distracted."

I looked into her eyes and said:

"We shed our tears upon this battlefield as we watch the tide of death take many out to sea. Yes, today we are forced to face the collective projections of life that is going wrong. Those who can hear must arouse their hearts and hearken to Truth for if they do not wake up fast they shall drift into a collective nightmare.

"This is the cost of a society heedless to the truth of the times and a people that have strayed into apathy, materialism and blind indifference.

"A world that has fallen deep into self-absorption wherein everyone has become so confused, weak and powerless."

She answered: "What you say speaks to my heart but it is so hard. Humanity has become so psychologically sick there is not enough true light to discharge this rising madness. The burden seems too great.

"I feel we have been abandoned by our elders and left to fend for ourselves in a world that has lost all hope and meaning. We are a targeted and easy prey for this ruthless, material civilization that exploits its children to fatten itself.

No one wants to listen; no one seems to care."

She looked away, down over the traffic.

I replied: "It takes a strong heart and mind to wade clear of this madness that threatens to claim us all. The cross of humanity is very heavy and this world seeks to deny its conscience by silencing the true servers of the race.

"In their denial they have burdened their children under the weight of the age."

I took her hand, "but remember…great are the forces of Love that lie beyond the periphery of human sight, humanity's true guides are ever present. They shall always aid those whose hearts are sincere. I smiled softly.

She whispered: "But humanity is living heedless to what is transpiring.

"Deaf and inert do they live their lives. Their hearts so dull, their heads filled with so many trivial and dead things.

"They have become so lost that they know not they are."

Fire flashed behind her eyes. "This world shall not claim me!" she responded defiantly.

I smiled at her bravery. "It is living intuitively and selflessly that is true rebellion in a world twisted in lies, selfishness and deceit. We must live from our true centre of being should we withstand this illusion as the world does roar.

"Collectively, we are now being forced to face the

self-created demons of our past as this juggernaut of civilization rises and what we have unleashed seeks to draw us into conflict and war.

"We must face this openly, honestly and bravely."

She looked out into the distance.

"Within my heart there are visions not of this world. A remembrance of the Greater Life arouses from within. I have a call to inspire and awaken those who smother this sight by their own hands and foolishness."

I whispered: "Trust in the guidance of your heart and live your life selflessly, in such a way as to invoke that true grace that seeks to help you.

"Let your writing be, as your soul guides to serve the race.

"In a time of confusion and world deceit you have the true honesty to confront those self-deceptions within and around you. You arouse those sleeping hearts to their true divine nature. That is rare and to live in such a way takes a selfless heart."

Together we looked out beyond the smog hazed horizon.

Her voice broke, "but sometimes I feel so alone…"

I put my arms around her and a soft vibration of divine Love rippled the ethers around us. It touched her heart and she swelled with grateful tears.

I smiled. "No, you are not alone and when your work here is finished the Kingdom awaits you…"

Such A Strange Thing

It is such a strange thing
To be here, in this dying dream.
Each day before these weary eyes
Flash images of a world that has disappeared,
Like a projector wheel unwinding.
We walk amongst you
Scattered fragments placed in a foreign world
In a history that is not our own
How can we explain
That which you cannot know?
Unearthly lights walking amongst the blind,
A collective recovering its memory
That its truth lies not here
Remembering that which was always ours
Dying to a world that never was.
To fulfil that which has already come to pass
For what must be has already happened
Within the cosmic heart,
And though it is unwise to indulge in perplexity
Many of us are startled

As the Shadows Play Around Us

That we passed by you unheeded,
For a Divine offering has been given
Which you have mocked
And from which you have turned away,
A life raft rejected from the drowning.
Now, time like sand is slipping through Love's fingers
And Gods hand shall be revealed;
Shall you find yourselves within Love's palm
To be lifted safely to the Great Mother's heart?
Or shall you forfeit true life
Wailing in chaos and shame?
We see your darkened eyes
And they reveal your choice,
Such is the sadness of Christ

It is such a strange thing
To be here in this dying dream…

The Selfless Flower

There was a young lady who climbed a mountain.

Her ascent was hard and lonely as she battled against the cold hard winds that constantly wanted to tear her down.

Finally she reached a plateau, high above the villagers who gossiped about her, below her.

Scarred and cut, battered and bruised, she looked out to the horizon and smiled.

It was here she would plant her garden.

From the mountain she took her stone and erected her walls.

With her soul she laid the earth.

With her love for life she gathered her seeds.

And with the fondest touch she planted them.

But with the highest of altitudes, harsher was the climate that fought her, made more miserable by the wind-lifted mockery of the villagers' laughter that assailed her.

Exposed to those battering winds and bitter colds she struggled to bring life where there was so little.

Weathered she became, as many years went on, but this hardened her will to keep her garden safe from the elements that sought to destroy it.

And endure she did.

Kept going by the warmth of her heart, she watched the seeds slowly sprout.

But those seeds were young and fragile and many died, killed by the ever-growing weeds amongst them, for she had not the strength to save them all.

There were some that budded only to be torn from the ground, lost to the cold harsh wind when she was not looking, too busy trying to save others.

There were those that flowered, opened by her loving kiss, blossomed by her loving touch, but cry they would when she pruned them, unable to understand her intention to help them grow higher and flower brighter.

Still she nurtured and toiled.

But as years went on, old she became and her strength she lost, for with all that she gave it her garden gave little in return.

Only glimpses of colour and a sudden waft of loving scent but flourish it did not.

Then one morning she woke to find a frost had stolen the life from it all.

Broken and disgruntled she fell to the lifeless soil and wept.

Drained was her spirit and she knew she had not the strength to start again.

It was then a bee, who had been watching from her wall, flew down to rest on the end of her finger.

"Why is it that you weep?"

As she sobbed, "for my garden has gone and empty is my breast, for my very heart has gone into this dry, dead soil and I cry for all my effort has been in vain."

It was then the bee smiled.

"Go to your walls and push them down."

And with the last of her strength she did.

As they collapsed around her, she fell to her knees in awe; beyond her garden the mountain bloomed in flowers with more radiance and love than she could ever imagine.

And the bee whispered: "Upon your wall I have sat and watched you for many years. I have watched you struggle in your garden with devotion and enduring love.

"I have watched your flowers grow with only the smallest of thanks for the sacrifice you gave them. But I saw the seeds of your love fly beyond your walls and flourish where you could not see them.

"Stop and listen to the world around you; there is peace, for long ago the laughter stopped.

"The villagers that once mocked and chastised you are now humbled as their children frolic and play in the miracle you have created.

"Take a walk within the garden of your love, my giver of life, and look inside yourself.

"You will find the most beautiful flower of them all.

"It is called the selfless flower.
"It is yours."

Chops

It was my friend Dreamer who warned us.

One morning he awoke bleating in terror. "A storm is coming, a storm is coming and it is the horse that draws Death's chariot. Take me to the Rams so I might warn them."

The lambs laughed and the ewes told him not to be so silly.

Dreamer had always been a weird little lamb. Most of the flock avoided him and he avoided most of the flock. Preferring the company of solitude, he usually sat alone in the quieter corners of the paddock. Even I, Split Hoof, gave him plenty of distance for when I would ask him to play he would just frown and tell me not to be so stupid.

That was why I was so taken aback by his outburst.

Realising his cry had fallen upon deaf ears he turned about and went to the Rams.

Curious, I followed at a distance.

The Rams all frowned at his approach; it was unusual for a lamb to enter their feeding circle.

Dreamer walked into its centre and spoke to them.

"A storm is coming; it is the horse that drives Death's chariot. It is time for us to seek refuge elsewhere."

At this, some of the Rams broke into laughter, though most didn't even look up from the grain bin. Then Blockpusher, the loudest of the flock spoke: "How do you know it comes my little friend?"

"I can smell it," Dreamer spoke earnestly.

The Rams all laughed and pretended to sniff the air and Blockpusher spoke again: "It is funny that I do not; I have sniffed many a storm before."

"That is because you use your senses and not your sense," Dreamer answered.

Then the Ram Readalot butted in. "Listen my little lamb," as he winked to the others, "for many years I have lived in this paddock. Like you, when I was your age, I also held these same fears until one day I realised that it was foolish wasting my life worrying about it, so I lived it. That was many years ago and all of us here have endured many a hard season. What makes you think that this one will claim us?"

Dreamer frowned, "Because this is the storm we have asked for."

"Why would we ask for that which could kill us, my confused little lamb? You would have us leave our beloved paddock and follow you, a lamb, into the woods to be savaged by wild dogs and hell knows what else? Go back to your friends, go back to your playing."

Dreamer spoke forcefully. "With your contempt you

have called for results and soon they will be given. I DO NOT ask that you follow me nor anyone else for that is the very reason why Death comes to claim you. I plead that you listen to the cry of your heart so you follow its song, let it take you to greener pastures. In our own ignorance we have forgotten that we are just sheep."

Readalot grew angry. "Listen to my heart, such rubbish you speak. You, lamb, have the arrogance to tell us we are mindless sheep; you have a lot to learn you contemptuous little dropping. Best leave here before we kick you silly."

The other Rams shook their heads in disbelief.

Dreamer snapped: "You have the arrogance to say you are not."

Then he sighed and looked around the circle to stop at each Ram as he went around. "Now, as I stand in the presence of you all, I see what has happened. How can one listen to his heart if its sound is smothered by the sound of his own loud voice? I shall pray for you all because I see death in your eyes. His stench rides the breath of your own self-deceit; you are so proud as to be stupid."

"That is quite enough!" a voice called from the rear of the grain bin. It was Greybeard, the oldest and most respected of all Rams. "I have heard many such heretical cries of prophetic doom over the years, the lunatic fringe is always spawning such wicked yarns; best we just turn our back on our psychotic little soothsayer here. He is just a foolish little lamb."

Then the Ram Praysabit spoke. "He has forgotten about the farmer who has fed and kept us all our lives. He will save us; I have faith in him."

"The farmer you pray to is an idol and a lie; your faith is justification of your own wickedness," Dreamer bleated.

"You curse at the farmer, you ignorant little devil," yelled Praysabit, "he who has given us the benefit of his technology.

"Thanks to him our grain bins are never empty and we are never hungry. Thanks to him our dams are always full so we are never thirsty; praise for him who built this fence to protect us from wild dogs."

"How could you insult him? Have you no sense of morality? You are mad!"

Dreamer spat: "That is what has damned you. He has poisoned you and you love its taste. Contentment has made you arrogant, laziness has made you sleepy; how can you call me ignorant when it is you that speak from a dream? The paddock is barren and your children are restless: they butt out their frustrations on each other. High on fungus and hollow thrills, they commit crimes of emptiness and don't know why. They feel an invisible hand around their throats and do not know whose hand it is. All are crying for answers. Answers that you have forgotten from a truth that you have turned your backsides to, for your heads are in the grain bin.

"The fence that protects you sentences you, for it cannot protect you from yourselves. Your poisoned minds are left to their own poisonous devices. The farmer has done his job well." Dreamer held his ground.

The Rams turned around and pointed their dags at him. Then, with a solid smack, Greybeard kicked him out of the circle. "You have gone too far lamb; you are banished from us."

Dreamer rose to his feet and went to speak but the sheep laughed at him; using their bodies they pushed him from the flock. Dreamer bleated, "HOPE HAS TURNED TO DECEIT AND LOVE HAS GONE SOUR"!

From a distance I had heard it all. I trotted myself over to him and he spoke to me. "Split Hoof, my friend, will you not come with me?"

Shaking my little horns I declined. "Though I am lame and an outcast like yourself, I will follow the flock because it is all I know."

"Then I must say goodbye and pray that your lame leg saves you. Hope has turned to deceit and love has gone sour. Beware the great fog my friend.

"For when a sheep has turned arrogant, too long it has been since it has seen a wolf. So when they stand in the open, bleating loudly their self-importance, they are wingless flies demanding a hungry spider to come pay its respect.

"I say the wolf has answered."

Climbing to his hooves he said, "goodbye and may your leg fail as they run towards certainty". Then he trotted away.

Many days passed. The flock enjoyed poking fun at the words of Dreamer. Many said he would come back but as days turned to weeks I knew he was gone forever. Many said the wild dogs had savaged him, many just said he was mad.

Weeks turned into months and many a lovely day went by until one day a strange thing happened.

Bored, I sat watching the sheep grazing, mounting and sleeping and a question formed upon my lips, WHY? But as soon as it came I lost it and suddenly I couldn't recall who I was. I asked the herd but the lambs all laughed and the ewes just bleated, "Split Hoof, you silly lamb".

But that was not enough; something was missing but I couldn't think what it was. Grey was all around me and I felt suffocated.

The Great Fog was upon me so suddenly that everything went black and then I realised it had always been there. My whole life I had been wandering aimlessly.

I tried to recall the last time I had seen the sun but I had forgotten what it looked like.

It was so dark that no one could tell the left from their right or right from wrong and the sheep just kept on grazing, oblivious to the floating death around them.

Panicking, I screamed: "REMEMBER DREAMER, REMEMBER DREAMER. The Rams just frowned; they hadn't noticed anything. The lambs all laughed and the ewes just called me silly.

Shaking in fear, I lay down and closed my eyes. Letting go to fear, I wanted death to just take me. Then, suddenly, a light lit from within and I could see.

I yelled to the flock: "The paddock is an ideal of freedom that has led you to bondage; let it go we must seek higher ground."

The flock laughed and I then knew that I would have to go alone.

Climbing to my hooves, I looked around and found a path in the darkness. It went beyond the fence to higher ground and I let the song of my heart guide me. I climbed up the hill until I found a stable ledge and there I sat overlooking the paddock, quietly overseeing them all.

As days went by I noticed a change in the flock. One by one some of the sheep would wake up screaming.

"I am blind," some would bleat. "We are dead," bleated the others, and I could tell that the fog had claimed them.

Those that panicked ran into the fence, hanging themselves on barbed wire; those that cleared it ran blindly into the unknown, food for wild dogs. Some went mad eating fungus.

I would cry out to them but lost in such fear they could not hear me. I saw death coming in the distance and I saw the storm over us all.

The Rams stood around the grain bin oblivious to everything but their own loud voices. The ewes stood by the Rams; the lambs stood around the ewes. Doom hugged them all.

Then the rains of confusion started and the sheep pulled together to keep warm. "It's just a little rain," laughed the Rams. "Nothing to worry about."

But that little rain turned into a great rain and the paddock began to flood. One by one they began to take notice; one by one they realised they were all in darkness and tighter they drew together. "Safety in numbers," one of the ewes cried.

But it wasn't until the grain bins flooded that the Rams grew nervous.

"Don't worry," Praysabit assured the flock, "the farmer will save us," though he did not sound so sure of himself.

Still the rain kept coming and the Rams began to panic; finding themselves in the great fog, they began to scream. Everyone went crazy.

"We are doomed," screamed the Rams as they trampled the ewes.

"We are all going to die," screamed the ewes that smothered their lambs. "Every sheep for himself."

Fights broke out everywhere as the Rams used their horns to kill the weak, standing on the bodies of others to keep themselves from drowning.

From my little island I watched in horror as dead lambs floated past me. I could hear the cries of the ewes and the panic of the Rams. I heard some of them cry, "pray for the farmer, pray for the farmer", and many bowed their heads in prayer. It was then lightning flashed and thunder answered. I heard a howl in the distance.

Suddenly a car horn beeped. "The farmer is here," Praysabit bleated, as the choking of an engine sounded over the rain.

The sheep all cried with joy. "We are rescued, praise the farmer."

The farmer gave a long whistle to follow his ute; the Rams leading the way as the flock ran towards him.

I followed, but my lame leg gave out from under me. Stuck in the mud, I raised my head, helpless! It was then I noticed something was wrong. I could smell it. They were all in such a rush they did not notice.

Limping behind them, I realised I could not catch up. "Come back," I cried but the rain had drowned out my voice and they were too far away. "Come back."

The Rams all cheered as the farmer opened the doors to the Big Red Shed and all the sheep filed in. Warm and safe inside, the Rams regained their composure.

"I told you there was nothing to fear," spoke Greybeard. "I knew the farmer would save us," laughed Praysabit.

All the Rams admonished the flock. "We told you we were right," and then the farmer entered the shed and shut the doors behind him.

Turning around to bleat their thanks, one of the ewes started screaming as the farmer tipped up his hat to expose his shadowed face.

Putting on an apron, the wolf picked up his meat cleaver and howled.

Outside the slaughter house I sat and listened to the screaming. Hearing footsteps behind me, I turned around to see Dreamer smiling-sad and knowing.

"I tried my hardest," was all that he said as we walked through sunny fields and I nodded my head. "I know you did my friend, I know you did."

Gaia Laments

The flash and terrible roar
Of a great star fallen,
The anguish
Of countless worlds
And beings
Drawn into chaos
And cosmic illusion.
Behold the blue jewel
Stolen and consumed
Raped by malefic intent,
Her children
Cast into darkness
Lost in forgetfulness
Infiltrated and grafted
Through time and space
To cosmic misery
And terror,
And Gaia laments
The song
Of her broken heart

As the Shadows Play Around Us

Ripples through the cosmos,
Her burden too heavy
As she resigns to futility
And we shudder
At the great travesty
Befallen her.

In answer to her cry
We came to this world
Fracturing unity
Descending
Through vibration
Imprinting ourselves
Upon shadow;
Threads of light
Anchored to earth
To consummate life
Seeding the planet
In joyous union
And in answer
To her prayer
Many have come
To witness this event
From other worlds
Spaces and densities
Places unseen
And unknown
Quivering in hope

Warren Sunkar

And anticipation
For what does come
Shall reach far beyond
This little world
And the dweller here.

And for a moment
We stand amongst you
Waiting, suffering
Wanting in expectation
Heaven does come to earth
And the great fire
Shall descend through us
But a flash in time
And a bend in space,
Yet a memory
That shall burn
In your hearts forever
For now Gaia awakes
Opening, yearning
Unfolding to rise
Into the arms
Of her lover
And all shall share
In her blessings hereafter.

Behold the blue angel
Shining in the firmament.

Through the Veil

As I sat on a park bench under the dim glow of a terrace street light, Asha walked over to me.

The deep and heavy problems of this wayward world often weighed heavily upon her heart. Often we would seek the sanctuary of each other's company in the night and under the stars.

Staring into the darkness we held each other's hand as we contemplated a tired and outworn humanity. A world, merciless and harsh. A people so lost and yet so arrogant. A society that was so loud yet so afraid.

Today, we could see a collective that had become imprisoned within its own self-created madness, running into the dark chasms of its own repetitive and bloodied past. Here were a people unheeding of the signs that flashed blatantly before them...

Her eyes glistened with tears as she softly let go of my hand.

"The people of this world are like caged animals that have forgotten that which lies beyond their bars. I feel their pain and separateness, yet, should I reach out my hand in love they would only swipe at me in fear," she softly cried.

I looked at her. "I know why you cry, for I too shed the same tears. Humanity has lived heedless of truth and that which has been forewarned.

"Now they begin to tremble before that which they have created."

She whispered: "Great is the pressure upon their hearts and minds as the Divine Fire bears down. Unwilling to face their true predicament many are burying themselves deeper in their illusions. This is only creating great pressure and engendering greater fear. Deaf to true guidance, possession grips this world. Now it shall break into madness."

She looked up into my eyes. "Why do they fail to see the truth? That until all this egotism is conquered, the door of life will remain shut. Until the prince of this world is brought to his knees, the transcendental shall remain hidden and inaccessible. Divine Love will not find its way into the hearts of men!"

"Yes," I smiled weakly, "hiding in the darkness humanity revels in its madness! As the world ego struggles against itself, despair and anxiety grow. This is the product of those who stand in fear of life, ignorant of truth. Pushing their denial into extremities, they will continue to spiral downwards into increasing fear and negativity. It is under cosmic impetus that all is being brought to the light and now there will be no place to hide as global processes accelerate and this degenerate civilization is brought to its end. The Divine Fire will purify this world!"

"Yes", she answered, "driven back by the fire of Love the world ego faces its death. Hard are the realisations to be faced by those who can heed the truth of these times…as we must now struggle through the madness of this world."

She looked at me helplessly. "This dying world order struggles to maintain its rotten existence instead of submitting to Truth, humanity in its blindness would rather run to conflict and annihilation!"

I answered: "Yet by facing death itself humanity could release those qualities of heart and soul that they have buried under all their lies and deceit to understand that which is real.

"If those who could but hear and understand the real liberation in truly confronting such an event, they would realise that it is time to face that which must be faced and to seek the essential. Then the false glitter of this fallen world will lose its attraction and the Truth within them could be revealed.

"Then many could understand that beyond the veil of death even within all this madness…Love is waiting!"

She took my hand, "we must not partake in the growing insanity but shall bare the harsh reality and affliction of this hour. Love does summon and we are ever led onwards."

"Yes", I replied, "do not fear, we are called within an hour seemingly bereft of light yet it is within this darkness that the Truth calls to those sparks that seek the greater communion. Today, only those pure of heart can heed and respond to such a call."

Looking out into the darkness she sighed: "How do we stand within such madness?"

Taking back her hand, together, we fell on our knees in supplication.

Looking upwards towards the heavens did we still our hearts and minds as the shadows of the world danced and played around us.

Surrendering within, in the darkness of the night did the veil of death dissolve as the Light Supernal descended upon us.

Thy will be done…we prayed in the deepest silence of our hearts.

The Dawn Lovers

One night, at a village feast held in honour of his return, Seth the poet left silently into the dark night, leaving the loudness and drunken festivity behind him.

Watching him quietly disappear, his beloved childhood friend Alexandra followed him into the garden. She found him alone and sitting under the luminous moon. Sitting down beside him she took his hand. "Why do you sit out here alone?"

He looked into her eyes and smiled.

"I sit by myself but never am I alone. Tonight I share the darkness with a bird whose cries echo throughout the valley and whose call beckons me to open my wings and fly with him. I sit by myself because who would sit with me and enjoy simple pleasures?

"Not they," as he pointed to the drunken and loud figures raising mugs behind them.

"You judge them harshly," she frowned, "they are your friends and they celebrate your return."

His face grew hard. "They celebrate themselves for

themselves; I am but an excuse for their own debasement."

Then his face softened as he explained. "They know not Love, only its pollution and those who don't know Love cannot know Life. Those that don't know Life cannot find Love, so they are friends to no one.

"They would rather sing their drunken songs of ignorance than listen to the truth. They would rather glut their senses in the presence of themselves than break simple bread with a stranger.

"They would rather pass out on wine than battle sleep to watch the sun rise. They would always rather something for themselves."

Alexandra sighed. "What you say may well be true but that is no reason for this self-imposed exile. There is no sense in your solitude. Join us back at the table."

Then Seth squeezed her hand. "Should you talk to me in reason then I will not answer because you cannot hear. Let us leave sense and its absurdities with the drunkards inside for they will tell you that they have it and that I am mad. Here under the moonlight I sit at a table of beauty, in there I sit with emptiness."

He looked out into the night and whispered: "You say it is I who sit in solitude but I say take a look behind you. You will see who has cut off their connection to love and you will realise it is not I who is in exile and it is not I who am mad. It is they. They who mask their tears under a veil of drunkenness."

Then she looked back behind her…

That night two childhood lovers wrapped in each other's arms battled sleep to watch the sunrise.

So Does A Lie Meet Its End

You have erected great cities
Concrete, metal and bold
Tall buildings and structures
Which are but tombstones
Offset a smoking horizon
A subconscious defiance
Upon the cusp of great change;
Children at play
In their own graveyard,
A people reflecting
Their hardened hearts
And rigid minds
Unwilling to let go
Unable to open
Trapped in a decaying thought
Which they will not repent.
It is but a civilization
Breathing its last breath
Not unlike worms
Feeding upon a corpse

As the Shadows Play Around Us

Your priests
And your prophets
Chant mantras of death
Beating upon a drum
Estranged
From the cosmic pulse
Attuned
To the sickened heartbeat
Of fallen life
In which you are all but devils
Dancing in a ring
Of false light
Prostrating yourselves
Before a shadow
A black and unholy creation
Which has turned upon you
And made you its slave.
Oh, hypocrites and fiends
Betrayers of Life
Servants
Of the defiled Word
Generation after generation
You have thrown your children
Upon an anvil
To beat in your masters will
Forging them to a program
Of a tortured and twisted mind

Warren Sunkar

Burning in the fires of hell
A lineage of death
Begotten of the great beast
That eats its own children
And has usurped your hearts.

Planning, plotting
Scheming and deceiving
Is the antichrist
Working inside you,
A wayward intelligence
That would rationalise
Its own madness,
An arrogance
That would stamp its mark
In time
In defiance of change
But a great desperation
And effort of futility
In this dark ocean
Of impermanence,
And behind your eyes
Shine its darkened will
And your smiles
Are but a thin veneer
Of hypocrisy
That would veil
An amalgamation

Of lies and deceit,
Such is the terror of a lie
Afraid of being unmasked.

Take heed, oh humanity
To this living testimony
Of the immovable race.
Silent Witnesses
Standing amongst you
Of an event that you are in
But will not see,
A world at war
With its own soul
Defying its conscience
The great battle being played
Within the hearts of men
Now as Judgement draws near
We ask you,
Must our cry be in vain?
For we see
That you shall cling
To a reality false,
To this illusion enforced
By its own denial,
An old and crumbling house
That you will not leave
Though its foundations are shaking
Upon a ledge

That can no longer support
That shall have you tumble
Into an abyss.

For though your world
And your dreams
Lay in waste
You have spurned
The offered hand
And revel like swine
In a dung heap,
And now we must watch
As your world
Crumbles around you
Knowing that you
Make your dying stand
Upon the very quicksand
That shall consume you.
And so does a lie
Meet its end.

The Graveyard Vagabond

I walk in a land of ghosts.

In a city of gravestones, I hear their cries in every word they don't speak and feel the pain in every word they do. It is a pain that burns forever within my chest because I know loneliness is an unquenchable fire. They hide in the shadows of a broken heart and cry for help but it is futile because in a world of darkness no one can find each other.

I walk in a land of ghosts.

Who whisper words of love but how can one talk of love when they draw it from an empty well.

Who use words of trust but they are disposable for they have become disposable people. They search for meaning in the meaningless and cry murder when the loving truth lets the lie kill itself because they realise that without their lies they have nothing to protect themselves with, and by destroying the truth there is nothing to remind them of who they really are.

I walk in a land of ghosts.

Empty like the land I visited before this one, for

everywhere they have sucked Mother Earth's teat of all its richness and turned it into cancerous bile.

They portion it out as medicine but grow more sickly every day. Like lepers, they watch each other fall to pieces. Sweeping their digits under the carpet, they smile their toothless smiles as if nothing is wrong. Those that are born with disease only know disease…that is their legacy to their children.

Cursed with life, I walk amongst the dead, kissing the lips of corpses. Trying to resuscitate those who will not be saved. I watch their restless spirits rattle their chains, and I hear their cries for salvation when I walk past. But I cast my eyes down because they can't stand that I can see right through them. They look at me strangely when I ask them to awaken because they do not know they are in a dream gone bad.

I think they hate me.

And how can I blame them.

For how can one not offend shadows when one tells them they have no substance in this shadow world, and how can one not expect the gravest misgivings when one talks about light and they can only picture darkness.

Best I stay silent and keep walking.

Truly, I am an outcast in this strange, ghostly land.

Unutterable Love

As these weary eyes
Look over this darkened world
The wails of existence
Assail these ears.
Separate, isolated, confused
Must one traverse this veil of tears.
Humanity how you struggle
To shield the Truth from sight
Keeping each other cursed
In this never ending night.
Beloved Father,
Help me to let go
Of this sufferance of life,
I know this world is but a hell
Of confusion, pain and strife.
We are lost in this realm
Of unquenchable fire
Chained to these planes
By burning desire.
Do we sustain our own cause

Warren Sunkar

At the cost of all
Every day in this prison
To re-enact the great fall.
Oh, Aurora of Love
Shine Through the window of this soul
Take me in thy Caring hand
Unmake me so I can be made whole.
Claim me, loving Father,
Anoint me with your fiery Kiss
I'm unable to deny you
Not wanting to resist.
Oh, how this heart yearns
For such glimpses of light
And touches of grace
Boundless, transcendent, supernal
Before time, beyond space.

Unutterable Love
Christ calling me
Dissolve me in your radiance
To die to thee.

The Heart That Searches

One night my heart pulled me to a lonely glade on the top of a hill. In the shadows of a great tree I heard the crying of an old and heartbroken poet. Stopping at his side I sat down next to him and asked him: "What is so sad that makes a man bleed his heart's final beats into emptiness?"

His world-weary eyes raised to meet my own and cast such a stare that my soul buckled with its heaviness. His whiskey-stained voice rasped as he held out a tear stained piece of paper in his scarred and wrinkled hand.

"This was to be the script of a boy who set sail upon the tide of his dreams and conquered the world's pain with love and youthful passion. Now it is but a scribbled page, unfinished and dirty for the boy has returned a man, lost for words and full of painful memories. Now he faces death, fearing and ashamed, for he has done nothing but sit in the shadows of men preaching to the world from an empty bottle what it could have been, if only it had followed him but then he realised that the world had and that was its problem."

Sobbing into my shoulder his voice broke, "I have travelled so far only to find I know so little. I am to leave a fool and a failure."

With a comforting hand over his shoulder, I smiled. "You speak such ugliness in the presence of such beauty."

His brow furrowed as he croaked in disbelief. "You speak of a beauty I see not; reveal its face so I may trace its lines with word in pen."

"Then trace the lines of your own heart, the heart that searches, for its journey is the song on the lips of every living creature. Worry not, that your prose be unfinished because it is complete. Worry not, if your words are illegible or misspelled, these are words of your heart.

"Let every phrase glitter like the stars in the night sky and light the path of those who wander. Let the sailor set his course by the light you give him, and let your love steer him clear of the reefs and whirlpools that claim the unweary, for many will sail the ship of truth to foreign shore.

"Let your pain be an offering to those who wish to avoid heartache, expose your scars so that those who wish to be villainous rethink their values as to avoid the karmic whip. You have laid in the dirt so others who walked over you kept their feet clean. That is the love that cries on my shoulder this very moment, the very love that cares enough to think he has failed. Go my friend for there are arms waiting to embrace you; release your hold on sorrow and fly beyond pain."

As the Shadows Play Around Us

His head in my arms I watched death steal his fire with a stilling kiss and I closed my eyes and held his hand for I, too, knew the loneliness of sobriety.

The Ark of Christ

Behind the veil
Unseen by mortal eyes
A silent community
At labour
In the field
Of the Lord.
Attuned to another existence
A living body
In this field of death
Resolved to place themselves
In the light of Christ
To erect a great
Citadel of truth
Within this stronghold
Of darkness
Charged to gather
A harvest of souls
Salvaged from this
World of illusions
We have come

As the Shadows Play Around Us

As strangers amongst you
Unheard and unseen
Placed upon foreign soil
Standing estranged
And in silence
Behind clashing
And contending tides
As the dark ocean
Swirls and swells.
And the cry for liberation
Raises and resounds
From the frightened and weary
Upon dualistic earth
For humanity is caught
In a rip and a play
Of cosmic illusion
Under the dominion
Of demonic and titanic forces
Such is the great
Travesty and truth
Of sensual reality.

At the end of this age
The mysteries of God
Stand revealed,
The keys of new life
Are thrown at your feet
And we stand as one

Warren Sunkar

Pillars of Love
Upon a foundation
Of universal truth
Redeemed through
The blood of Christ
Charged to gather
The remnants of the Living
And prepare the way
For the coming
Of the Lord
For as the dawn breaks
We crow as harbingers
Of the new day.

Oh warriors of virtue lost
Oh pilgrims compelled
By the inner sun,
Can you fathom these words
And know this revelation;
Are you able
To disassociate
With fallen life
And lift your eyes
To the hills
From whence comes
Your salvation?
Will you lay yourselves
Upon the altar of Love

And come share
In our great labour,
You who are called
To new life
The hour has come
To confirm your election
And take thy place
Within this merciful imposition
Of divine wonder.

Oh Brothers and Sisters
Scattered and diminished
Throughout this world
You are charged
To unite in Love
Shake off thy dust
And present yourselves
Or slip into the darkness forever.
We stand as gates
And all those who truly seek
Shall come and find
And all who can
Shall enter
And know rest
From the great tempest
That Now, does come
For the cycle closes
And the precipitation

Of stronger current and force
Shall rain upon this sphere
Whereby the angel
Shall be raised
And the devil
Shall be swept away.

Oh Beloved and Elect
Stand strong and defiant
In this hour of evil
Lest you be caught sleeping
As the dragon does roar.
Endure this darkness
And know your redemption is near
For this world does rupture,
Let it not throw you
Off your feet
For sides are being chosen.
The foundations of Chaos
Are shaking,
The lines of demarcation
Are being drawn
And now the many shall come
Till the great advent
Upon the Day of the Sword,
And all shall know their fate
Within this final hour
Of the coming of the Lord.

ESOTERIC ARTICLES

Open The Window Of Grace

In this global society of technocratic convenience, entertainment and selfish distraction, how few people take time to still and truly gain the needed moments and space to open, bringing about the deeper inner clarity and transcendental awareness to assist a world that is seemingly spinning out of control? How few people even care or see the necessity of doing so?

Within today's great collective confusion and troubles, there is so much needed to be said about sacredness!

Sacredness reveals itself in the purity of relationships that are formed with God, ourselves and the planet. When we know true sacredness, we open our hearts and minds to the guidance and subtle caress of divine Life and we are drawn into Love's presence. Sacredness is the vehicle through which we come to understand our true nature and we come to realise that we are constantly showered with God's unspeakable blessings. Here in awe of Life we are constantly falling to our knees and can behold 'Truth Unmanifest' through our open window of reverence and love. Here, within the sacredness of a moment, Love manifests to touch our hearts as do the kisses of the morning sun's rays for those who awaken early to receive them.

It is through the portal of sacredness we experience a constant renewal in Life...

If you would but take that little time you have to contemplate this, you would understand that this is what lies in sacredness!

Sacredness is not an ideal or a concept. It is the inspired reverence you bring to the moment you are living. People should understand that true divine blessing can be experienced everywhere and in any situation but that we must offer ourselves up in sincerity and love. Sacredness is lived in the true recognition of divinity that pervades all form, through whatever place, being or moment we are interacting with. When Life is revered and we as a people come to honour each other in respect to our divine nature then this creates the opportunity for Spirit to teach and bless us. We then come to know Life consciously and know the purpose of our being!

Our modern culture for the most part has lost its sense of sacredness and does not recognise its importance. Without it, we lose our fundamental connection to essential reality and sensitiveness to those sublime understandings and elements that are given to us by Life to truly guide and nourish us. Without sacredness and respect for the divine Life we lose our spiritual guidance and begin to venerate matter and form. We become lost in dualistic reality and fall deeper into the illusions of self.

Today, this world has plunged deep into a material abyss of self-gratification, and we are seeing the direct results. In the degradation of true culture and our relationships to each other and the Earth, sciences and arts, potential tools used to elevate and enliven the race have become so polluted and degenerate their effect on society only weakens and defiles it. Driven by the chaos of their personal realities, people seal themselves from the true understanding of Life. This is true blindness!

When we lose sacredness we lose our divine compass and in our confusion we fall deeper from what sustains us. Our inspired recognition of the sacredness of Life opens the portal to higher dimensional reality. The opposite is also very true; in denial and negligence of Spirit we find ourselves lost in psychosis, trapped in misery and fear. As our society falls deeper into materialism and thus into madness we see the fires of hell arise around us in confusion, depression, vampirism and war.

We see this sickness arising in today's incessant push of those technocratic and inorganic pathways towards spiritless realities and worlds. Today our culture, has become a celebration of debasement and much of today's society is resembling the demonic stories of old!

Most people interact with each other and the planet

in a semiconscious daze, seeking only the attainment of their own desires and needs. Humanity is today cloaked with heavy insatiable elementals of their personality and it is here that they open themselves to be controlled by darker entities and beings. Collectively they are being driven off a metaphysical cliff to plunge into an even deeper abyss of hatred, conflict, and brutality...

Yet if we could only just open and trust our sense of sacredness it could elevate us far beyond the dangers and miseries of our prevailing conditions.

Let one here ask:

How few people today consciously engage in life with the love and clarity that is aroused by spirit?

How few people are even able to recognise the importance and necessity to see the sacredness of Life?

When you walk in nature do you take time to be still and feel her presence?

When you look into the eyes of the opposite sex do you honour their soul with your integrity and truth?

Is your walk through life attempting to live the deepest truths that reveal themselves to your heart, and how do you live behind closed doors?

When you know the sacredness in all things your answer will be without fear, confusion or hesitation.

Today as we watch in awe at that which is rising before us, let us see clearly the tragedy of our modern culture and look deep inside ourselves. Then we ourselves have the opportunity to see the sacredness of this moment in our planetary collective history. To turn this moment into the greatest of blessings and to meet divine Truth face to face. Then we can honour God, ourselves and our brothers and sisters by holding our alignment, integrity and truth before them. This is true divine work.

We must not only remember but live in sacredness... this moment is sacred, the Earth is sacred, humanity is sacred. When you know such a Reality and Love then your very lives become a divine blessing upon the world.

Verily, the whole cosmos will sing with you!

FALL ON YOUR FEET…NOT ON YOUR HEAD!

Our physical material world holds true potentiality as to our divine soul unfoldment as a species as well as contortions and distortions as to the nature of our collective journey through these realms and cosmos.

People need to wake up and pay attention for if we as a race seek to inherit our true divine birthright, it is important for people to question the direction in which we seem to be 'travelling'. This includes the possibility of contorted future incarnations as a collective into the 'realities' we are ourselves co-scripting.

Sometimes to see where we are going, one needs to know where they stand.

Ancient allegories, myths and stories have often related to humanity a collective event alluding to a fall of our collective being into realms that we as a race were premature to experience or possibly not even meant for.

Today many people are realising that somehow and

at some point, humanity shifted into identification with this physical material reality which is very far removed from the reality of our divine pre-history.

Gnostics have often hinted that what we perceive as the physical universe is in fact a realm in which humanity remains for the most part captive through a state of relativity and misidentification.

Through wrongful identification with our shadow selves (the personality/carnal nature/lower self) and misunderstanding the resonate field we exist within (duality), humanity has been able to deeply complicate its predicament by misuse of its forces and intelligence. Thus has the domination of our lower collective nature continue to involute to an ever deepening distortion of our 'reality'.

What has become known as The Fall still continues today!

As we seek to hold onto form life through our attention and identification at the expense of our divine nature, so do we corrupt our true divine potentiality.

The deeper complexities we will not get into in this piece! This is a somewhat simple explanation to a problem with real complexity and is but a loose conceptual framework to cast a little insight and light as to the extension of troubles we find ourselves in within our current collective situation.

However, despite what seems an impossible situation, divine servers have always subscribed that humanity does have a divine pedigree, and through our intrinsic nature we have the possibility to reconnect with our true divine reality and reawaken our divine beingness within this given organic matrix. Then through a transmutational and transfigurative process, we can move essentially to our original and destined vibratory reality.

Unknown to many upon the planet, this process has been happening throughout the ages by certain personages and groups who have embarked upon The Way and gone home. The teachings of the Avatars have been proclaimed throughout humanity's collective history and the way lived by those astute enough to heed the inner call of their true divine nature.

Today, should those of humanity heed their divine calling they will find they have their own inner co-ordinates and capability to transcend the current situation with much assistance from divine intermediaries and intelligence! Engaging consciously and actively as participants in the TRUE divine plan.

The purpose of this piece is not to inspire theological debate but to open enquiry as to our true nature and the importance of gaining a deeper perspective of where we are, what we are and where we might go – especially if we continue with our collective unconscious momentum and movement towards a transhumanist 'reality' that in truth, most of humanity has no clear inner perspective of.

As we neglect to heed true inner divine knowing and

proceed to venerate matter and form we continue to involute and reflect ever distorted realities back upon ourselves. In misusing our creational abilities we have the real potentiality to take ourselves further into realms far from our true divine reality and into states that are very hard to come back from.

To date, humanity has been aided by Divine Intelligence, enabling humanity to understand its time and space predicament and through its evolutionary capacities and sympathetic organic matrix enable it to find its way back home to its true divine cosmic origins. Our natural organic reality provides us with the means and opportunity to reawaken our divine potential and go the way home. However, through the domination of the lower mind and the misuse of our creative abilities, we lose our way and we now see a miscreant humanity seeking the total augmentation, control and blatant destruction of its organic reality.

Today's transhumanist 'reality' is but the deeper contortion and inversion of the true divine path and is but a signpost for a very hard and long journey back to our true divine home.

In these lower worlds we are subject to crystallisation, degeneration and 'I' sentiency. The concretion and adaptions of the lower mind lead to fundamental distortions as to our true soul identification and nature. With the loss of our inner knowing we are mostly unable to discern The Path and thus are subject to many confusions and distortions.

Today, society is experiencing an incessant push towards a transhumanist reality and new world order by certain individuals, groups and governments. As to the full agenda of these people who are guiding us towards these ends, we are as a race still relatively in the dark. Their tactics of subliminal manipulation, by-passing democratic processes and inhumane enforcement indicate their corruptive intent. The world ego with its 'established authorities' seeks to circumvent our inherent birthright having themselves misplaced their own identification with divine unity and lost themselves to involute pathways.

However today, due to the stimulation of the Earth and humanity by certain cosmic energies we are gifted with the possibilities of understanding and working with these in-flooding divine intelligences to co-creatively assist humanity with its re-identification to its true divine primordial unity! We have the potentiality to awaken from our misaligned perspectives into which we have fallen and to assist in the TRUE divine corrective process.

Here we need to shift our identification from our own personalised realities to our true soul nature.

Our biology and genetic potentiality flourish under the arriving waves of divine Love, awakening the consciousness of humanity. These new encodings are seeding the receptive, and new life is emerging. This is today being played out through the intensifying dramas of the world ego.

    It is time to embrace the change and your true inner potential...

False Offerings

Groups, organisations and people serving Life are only purposeful when they are acting in true response to the incoming light and revelation of the world soul. Truth, though ever immutable and unchangeable, is responded to accordingly through the variable conditions of fallen life and thus subject to change within the fluctuating conditions of response within the collective's outer dualistic mind. Thus, that which humanity finds truthful and purposeful today, becomes falsehood tomorrow. Those teachings that yesterday helped liberate the collective today turns to imprison it. The shifting sands of the outer conditions of earthly life change throughout its history as do the very winds that blow upon the Earth's surface.

At present there are many motivated individuals and groups, who, along the lines of earthly service, have falsely labelled, associated and even considered themselves to be the spiritual benefactors of humanity. Applying all and various, means and ideologies, to improve or save the planet via their own limited and personal views of truth, righteousness and what is good for the world. So idealistically and actively fixated upon the so-called good that they believe that they are doing, the call to new life is passing them by.

In natural worldly response, incarnated servers will always apply humanitarian standards of conscience within their earthly field of service. Such earthly goodwill is the sympathetic action of an open and loving heart to those base needs and requirements of existence in material life. However, such earthly service itself is not a means to an end.

Today many are caught or lost in the blindness and inertia of previous and truly unrealised spiritual teachings and outmoded impulses of yesterday, and are unable to intelligently or dynamically respond to the call of truth as it resounds within the present. The outer courts of this world are littered with such groups offering false hope, idealistic truths and redundant teachings that miserably fail in bringing divine Love to earth.

Few today are able or even willing to truly empty and still themselves, allowing the reorientation processes of divine Life to take them in hand and guide them as to what is truly needed to effectually bring about those necessary changes within earthly life and truly prepare as the great transition now speeds up hastily upon the outer planes of existence. Full of self, blind and unheeding do such beings chase their own tails within this labyrinth of dualistic life. For even with the best yet ignorant intentions such earthly or redundant offerings in effect are now truly denying that which is truly good and are doing great dis-service to all.

There are many conscious groups and individuals that lack true divine contact or experience, feigning light through false mystical occult practices and such dualistic activities – purposely leading astray the masses to suit their own intentions or fallen perspectives of truth – misguiding and confusing many while outwardly making displays of their service in false praise to God. These are the tenors of hypocrisy and behind them flourish the greater evils of the world. Verily, today, the call to new life goes mostly unheeded and the counterfeit spirit abounds.

Followers of older teachings should realise that such teachings are but the outward expression of the indwelling Life. Mere acknowledgement, affirmation of outward principles and attempts of self- transcendence through imitation has turned such teachings into the great parody and unfortunate burden that now weighs heavily upon humanity's shoulders. Without sound and true divine realisation such followers of their outer tenants are leading the world into great misfortune, further complicating the illusive conditions of a fast deteriorating world. Such teachings harnessed by those self-motivated individuals and groups to further their own designs are now having a definite and truly awful result upon the misguided and immature collective.

The true inner nature of the disciple or initiate is the ever yearning, thirsting and seeking indwelling soul, realising the true nature of dualistic life, crying for release. In truth there is but one offering that is necessary that opens the true way of initiation yet the ego would twist and contort such simplicity into all sorts of distortions, aberrations and concessions. The true required sacrifice that is to be offered upon the altar of Love is self! The many claims of initiation from such beings, affirmed by mental sophistry and cool self-determination, now, will not stand under the increasing pressure that the true life brings.

There is much talk and literature of a second coming, the coming one, planetary ascension. Such outer expositions have been quite dramatically and aberrantly twisted by the planetary ego to suit its own idealistic ways. Now it grapples with that which lies beyond its own twisted understanding. Few understand that divine Love will not find its way into human hearts until its outer courts are cleared personally and collectively. Until humanity truly yields up its idealisms and glamour, emptying itself of the false, can divine Love find its way into the collective human heart. Love will not enter a den of thieves.

The great contortion of truth within the mind and heart of humanity has made it almost completely unresponsive to the new call of Spirit today. Today love shall pass by the houses of many for none shall open the door.

Yet now as the Sword of divine Truth enters this world such beings and groups shall be exposed for what they truly are. The heavy yoke that they have placed upon humanity shall now be lifted as they and their false offerings are delivered to the shadows of redundancy. The light of divine Truth shall reveal those who would counterfeit the spirit and reveal the corruption that has grown within the collective's heart.

For with all said and done today evil is outwardly and openly flourishing and thriving on earth. Though symbols and words of love abound, such offerings are but the dualistic imposition of the perhaps well meaning yet unenlightened. Declarations of love and light propelled by self-will, blind belief and conviction have in effect done nothing to truly arrest the growing evil upon the planet and are simply impotent in effect and meaningless in bringing the divine plan into true manifestation.

Into the Dark Night

The lamentations of death compassed me about; the pains of hell surrounded me; I cried in my tribulation...
  A biblical quotation

There are definitive stages on one's spiritual journey when Life draws us deep into the dark and unfamiliar. The 'truths' and tangible relativities that we have created as sure footholds upon our imagined ladder of spiritual ascent start to crumble or dissipate into the inner spiritual void. The ephemeral and illusive qualities of what we thought was reality become apparent. We waver in the in-breath of the soul and our whole world begins undoing.

This is the dark night...

In this night we have moments of panic. We walk into it as the voices of unnumbered fears incessantly whisper to us to turn around and go back. In the darkness we lapse into moments of confusion as all temporal identifications are suspended and we desperately grasp at what we think we know. We try to hold on to those forms and ideals that have given us security and comfort as we navigate through the labyrinth of duality. Here we feel the futility and know the sad realisation that all that we thought we knew, all the insight we had gained, is nothing.

Intuitively we feel that the Dark Night is an invitation to a deeper shift in awareness but we are called into the dark with no signpost to guide or to point out the direction.

From those moments of inner confusion we look out into the world. We see its madness and our own. The wails of samsara assail our ears and the aridity of our existence dawns upon us as the suffering of those around us becomes apparent. We question our purpose and we recognise our loneliness and separation, feeling the pain of all those bound to the great deception. Life as we know it has no meaning, we have no meaning... strange and obscure reasoning arises.

As it gets to the deeper stages, we are in moments overwhelmed. How long must we endure, how much can we endure? We seek a means of possible escape but realise there is nowhere to go. We pass through terrible phases of fear, loss, panic and death. We have plunged into the depths and have lost all sense of up and down and feel like we are being held underwater. We are truly helpless and have lost all expectant hope and know only the denial of love.

And still it gets darker...

As we stumble through the greatest dark we cry out

in our torment. We writhe in anguish, with no balm to soothe our wounds or water to quench our parched lips. We wonder what we have done to be so denied of God. We are pushed to the depths of loneliness and despair... we fall to our knees as we struggle to understand what has bought us to such forsakenness?

This contemplation is not only dark, but also secret...St John of the Cross.

The secret of the dark night is one hidden in deep inner affliction. This is the grace of the deeper communion and unravelling into our inner unknowing. The true dark night is the communication of divine in secret, hidden from the self, purging us of all that hinders its expression. Its revelation must come through total self-abandonment as the deeper heart calls us into the darkness but only to deny us.

In the words of St John of the Cross...

"For this night is gradually drawing the spirit away from its ordinary and common experience of things and bringing it nearer the Divine sense, which is a stranger and an alien to all human ways. It seems now to the soul that it is going forth from its very self, with much affliction. At other times it wonders if it is under a charm or spell, and it goes about marvelling at the things it sees and hears, which seem to it very strange and rare, though they are the same that it was accustomed to experience aforetime. The reason of this is that the soul is now becoming alien and remote from common sense and knowledge of things,

in order that, being annihilated in this respect, it may be informed with the Divine."

As we traverse the way the experienced seeker will know many such nights. During these periods of dissolution one is asked to let go of all meditative work, all elusive seeking and that which might dupe the personality to focus upon itself during these times. Frustration, confusion and restlessness will only come as the result. Through the night we must let go of all that we think we are and these reflexes of self must be seen for what they are.

As our journey goes on, we understand that each night must get deeper and darker. The self often cries in pain of recognition as it enters the darkness knowing its trials, loneliness and frustration. Each entrance means a denial and a death. Yet in our emergence we begin to see with an ever deepening clarity that which we were blinded by and that we were kept from. We realise that all that we once were must be dissolved and discarded. Through our suffering, a deeper clarity and a deeper empathy is awoken from within and we see the arrogance of our ways and the futility of all that we have done.

Through each purgation we have visions and moments of unspeakable clarity as veils become transparent. The revelation of divine reality dissolves all hindrances to the deeper equanimity. The unknown stands revealed and expands into true realisation. The phenomena and false light of duality is seen as the illusive play that it is and all that has held us enamoured of this world is obscured...is blotted out by this dark love of God.

Seekers of Love, let it be known the path is often hard and has its perils. It should not be considered lightly. Upon the true journey home we have been warned by our elders of two dark stages, two great nights among many lesser ones. They are the deepest purgation of soul, and the darkest and most formidable night brings about a true union with the Divine.

Here upon the path of salvation, into the darkest of nights, is where the world is dissolved forever and our divine reorientation begins.

The way in which they are to conduct themselves in this night of sense is to devote themselves not at all to reasoning and meditation, since this is not the time for it, but to allow the soul to remain in peace and quietness, although it may seem clear to them that they are doing nothing and are wasting their time, and although it may appear to them that it is because of their weakness that they have no desire in that state to think of anything. The truth is that they will be doing quite sufficient if they have patience and persevere in prayer without making any effort....

The Dark Night of the Soul, St John of the Cross

The God of Illusions

Most of humanity looks out into the created universe today and imagines an omnipotent god controlling and governing the known universe. Those somewhat more spiritually inclined offer adulations and praise to this almighty creator and seek consolation when their lives are troubled or their understandings perplexed. Few seek the very foundations upon which they make their offerings from nor do they question the apparent chaos and disharmony that engulf them continually upon their short and somewhat miserable journey through this existence.

It is seen that humanity assumes much and yet knows very little as to the nature of its existence and its surrounding reality!

When people talk about God, do not they usually seek to understand a god of their own aspirations?

Is it not a reflection of certain qualities of their very selves, their hopes and desires that they project upon what God is?

The Christian church fathers tell us to place all

our trust in God and tell us that their god is all loving, all-powerful and all-knowing, and they, as servants of God, offer themselves to this almighty creator upon the foundations that their spiritual forefathers have stood.

Affirmed in their belief and worship by the mighty words of the avatars and saints that have appeared throughout humanity's collective history they have interpreted and attributed most of the given qualities to their god which they have learned through the guidance of the church and which the church itself has cultivated and reinforced over successive millennia.

So great are these attributes and so fervent in their belief they are that their followers simply do not question such a grand orchestration and authority. And over those successive generations they have worshipped such an image that it has become part embedded within their very blood consciousness. As many have given their devotion, time and even their lives to appease their god, in the church, today 'faith' is merely instinctual and their 'belief' automatic as it has become absorbed deeply within their racial consciousness.

Should we look back through humanity's collective history, its energetic investment in god over countless lifetimes is massive. Great battles have been fought in 'god's name' with conquests and conversions galore!

Countless martyrs have offered their own little lives to this great unknowable that somehow the church fathers seem to know all too well.

But what is it that humanity truly serves?

What happens when a people surrender their hearts and minds to such images as they personally and collectively continue to affirm their own ideals and beliefs to their very selves and each other?

Then through their maintained convictions dedicate their lives to that which they have been told, hope and even demand exists? Do they not through their own devices create a god in their own image?

Have they not projected and imposed their own will upon Truth?

And what of the strength of such an image when it has been cultivated over generations?

Can such a generated entity eventually dominate and overtake people's minds and hearts if they themselves exchange such falsehood over that which they innately sense is true and real – becoming the ignorant victims to such a reflected impression that has become governed and manipulated by an outside authority?

It is time that humanity understands what they serve and perhaps voice aloud those unutterable words that fear and self-deception fight against. Those words that will not be uttered by those who bare false witness to truth!

That we of ourselves know nothing!

Let us not be afraid to see that mostly the foundations of human worship to 'God' are illusory and even cancerous in their effect and to put it simply: Most of your spiritual leaders, priests and gurus have been self-deceived and they have been lying to you!

Here it must be said that with these words we do not want to stir or inflame passions against such personages. Such beings would not even hold any such positions of authority if the collective itself would not give them the energy to fortify themselves in their illusions and let it be seen that many such leaders are quite pure in their intent as they mostly believe with a conviction in what they teach and say.

The root of their lie exists not only within their minds but within their hearts and there it is fostered and reinforced every time they act discordant with the truth of their hearts and deny their true soul to serve the outward principles and values of their illusory authority.

When most people speak of god in a personal way they are prescribing attributes and terms as defined by their own relative perceptions, conceptions and experiences of life. An ego centred consciousness ascribes its reality in terms of personal understanding and relativity.

To an awakening or awakened heart and consciousness, the ego may be understood or known as the centre of fear, or the 'I' consciousness.

It is a disassociated aspect of our original and full consciousness that perhaps one could say is the microcosmic product of an aspect of our greater cosmic consciousness that fell beyond the relative measures of what humanity terms as time and space.

As a disassociated aspect of our original and full consciousness it perverts into a perception that draws itself deeper into its own version of a distorted and twisted reality.

As most of humanity draws its understanding and knowledge through individual perception and relativity, it is not wrong to say that most of people today are almost completely egocentric.

An egocentric consciousness is a limitation!

In fact, if it is strengthened and cultivated it can become a prison capturing a being in its own and partial version of temporal reality disconnecting them from higher aspects of reality, and when it has become a fundamental basis and identification of a being's existence, they have effectively shut themselves off from true reality and have fundamentally rendered themselves from life.

Such a rupture with the true centre of being is a death as darkness envelops the heart and fear is the result. From a more spiritualised perspective one could quite understandably term such a vehicle as the walking dead.

One could also describe those whose dominant facet of existence is living through and as an ego as those who are living in fear.

When someone has died in such a said manner all that they truly have is an illusion of life and thus it is not strange when one begins to awaken from their relative darkness that they cry out that all life is an illusion!

An illusion is a projection of fear, and in a personal

sense it is an image drawn from one's heart and mind to protect an ego from seeing the truth that is founded within the true centre of our being.

Those who live their lives purely egocentrically, live in and as an illusion. The ego itself cannot truly *know* anything but simply struggles to maintain and keep its existence thriving.

One of the curious survival impulses of a human ego is that it sees what it wants to see, hears only what it wants to hear and acts accordingly to what pleases and feeds it.

It mostly denies that which threatens its own interpretation of its illusory reality, thus its nature is averse to Divine Truth which it instinctually recognises as its enemy.

As a common defence a personality usually ascribes truth to itself and defends itself quite fiercely when it has been strongly cultivated and reinforced.

Turned outwardly into the phenomenal world, an ego asserts itself into identification with matter to affirm its reality and deny any inner impulse or call that might resound from Spirit!

Thus almost every impulse or desire that an egocentric and dominated consciousness acts upon or motivates is therefore usually in opposition to spiritual motive or awakening, and any truth, conception or ideal that it grasps upon of true divine reality is twisted, interpreted and reduced to its own personal perspective.

When such beings look out into phenomenal existence and surrender – attributing everything to their "God out there" – they have come to deny all that is truly real.

Having prostrated themselves before their god which is their inspired source of all their hopes, dreams and adulations, it is in truth their own individual and collective projection and reflection of fear. Such is humanity's great god of illusion!

Now when a divine personage appears or awakens upon the planet a great amount of true divine light and energy is radiated. At pertinent times in humanity's collective history the great ones such as Jesus, Gautama, Krishna and Mohammed have appeared as instruments of divinity to liberate those trapped divine sparks from their earthly prison. Well after they have departed from this world their resounding note and influence serves thousands of years afterward as a source of aspiration, inspiration and nourishment for entire civilizations.

Truly as one observes today's grand orchestration of religious institutions and cultural perspectives, one could say that such beings have made a great impression!

The light and impact that such a being brings to the collective is painful, burning through the layers of Maya, glamour and illusion that the planetary ego waxes around itself. While blazing a path through such density and darkness it stimulates, awakens and releases many divine sparks from their prison but it also provokes, disturbs and burns the planetary ego that often and usually reacts with great pain and distress seeking to muffle, restrain and even destroy such an intruder that it sees as the cause of its pain and becomes their adversary.

It is thus why all the great ones have faced such formidable trials, obstacles and much suffering in their service and dispensation of light and truth.

After such a divine personage has served their mission of true salvation and departed, the planetary ego instinctually moves to re-assert itself and is relatively swift and cunning in its response.

After a great one's departure the powerful and higher residual vibration and impression that such a being leaves upon the planet dynamically affects and impacts upon the remaining collective.

But such an impression must not be confused with the original and true divine salvific impulse which is received via the divine spark that lies at the true centre of one's being, which is the catharsis for true awakening and enlightenment.

It is but the 'bright shadow' that draws, affects and stirs the planetary ego in which it immediately seeks to utilize, to strengthen and reinforce itself! It is this false light that the planetary ego feeds and draws upon to maintain its illusory existence and empower its own twisted agenda.

Upon such higher impulses, energies and vibration that such a divine being leaves in its wake the world ego creates its own interpretations and images of divine reality, truth and god to pervert, seduce and overpower those of true humanity into wrongful identification.

It does this to draw and feed from their essence and projections to maintain its own illusion!

This is the greatly guarded secret and foundation that mainstream religion today refuses to admit as they are the keepers of the great illusion. That these unholy imitators of divine truth and life are merely serving to keep and maintain a shadow!

When we look out over the world today this is what we see.

A more awakened being shudders at the great delusions of mankind.

Cultivated over millennia, mainstream and organised religion is but a sickening parody far removed from the original salvific impulses and teachings that originally initiated them. Using the images of the great ones, the planetary ego has created many false gods.

Prostrating themselves before these degenerating images their keepers and their followers only serve to keep humanity locked in their earthly prison as they successfully dominate and control the planetary consciousness.

The great confusion and distortion of the true teachings from the great ones under mainstream and organised religion from the passing age is today but a great dragnet upon the collective.

Their followers blind and deaf, clinging to images that

lead astray, confuse and dominate many beings who are awakening to the new salvific impulse of the day!

They are lost in the refuse of the passing age and lack the innate ability, humility and honesty in the face of change as this world is put under increasing stimulation in accordance to divine decree.

As these cosmic rays of divine love and dissolution increase in their intensity formidable pressure is now to be continually exerted upon humanity.

Should humanity choose to remain fixed and unrepentant in its illusions, idealisms and ways they will suffer greatly by their own hands.

This has been forewarned by the various prophets, seers and divine beings throughout humanity's collective history, in which some have termed this tumultuous phase of great change Armageddon.

Those religious figures and keepers who continue to impose their evil authority and dominance upon the collective shall now be forcefully and finally thrown from their seats of power.

The glory and truth of the coming age has been greatly dimmed and distorted by those who would suffer others to their delusions, deceptions and self-gratifications.

Now in this final stage of the planetary corrective process those beings who refuse to align and submit to divine will and decree shall now be removed from this world as she awakens and moves on to her rightful place.

Darkness is Rising

Today darkness is rising and those of humanity who have the sight are able to see many foreboding and ominous signs of that which lies just ahead. Already many are feeling the great hopelessness and anguish that is resounding from the hungry Archonic matrix that fallen humanity exists within as it grows increasingly desperate and is fighting hard in the face of its rejection and subsequent destruction. Behind the face of what can only limply be called "civilization" great evil by those of the shadows is being wrought.

The presence of Greater evil that works insidiously behind civilizations face reveals itself not so much in those more obvious catastrophes and atrocities available to the public through its media but through truly abstract, degenerate and involutionary ways of collective living and sustainment. These are initiated and kept by those more sinister acts and occult means perpetrated behind civilisations face.

Those hidden things of which the public is naught aware yet are sustaining through their self absorption and ignorance. While suppressing all that is truly transformative, those who today govern the planet have invested greatly in perfidious means, methods and technologies which are mostly hidden from the public in preparation for this very hour. With means and intent to directly pervert that which is ordained by Divine decree for this planet.

Know whatever expression this great play of illusion and drama takes- all such effort shall come to naught at its end! For time is running out and while the elite and ruling over this world glutton themselves in their glorious moment of power and wealth, their dark masters shall now shake in understanding and despair in the realization that their time is done.

Today, the global totalitarian infrastructure that is emerging is no longer concerned in hiding itself. Propounding and propagating without concern its twisted moralities and obvious lies, neither does it harbor any real interest in the face of exposure or in any little resistance humanity might offer. It is a seemingly unstoppable juggernaut, rising to full expression, snapping its leash made from a thin and fast unravelling premise of decaying societal morality and denial. Those that occupy positions of authority and power in this vast and great hierarchy of lies are now beginning to reveal their nature as they are now unable to restrain their growing evil.

Thriving in their hierarchal reign of dog eat dog values, their truly false and mechanically rehearsed exterior values which are usually displayed for public conveniences are collapsing as are their governing systems and decaying ideologies.

The majority of Humanity has lost its cause and its voice having dived fast into an abyss of materialistic culture.

Fear is rising and brooding grows…it seems that humanity is steaming ahead upon a collision course with a miserable destiny.

A collapsing and suicidal global economy, a societal infrastructure that is fast degenerating and a world that is dying ecologically. Growing apathy, disease and collective depression are the ominous signs that society has lost its heart. Though the world's troubles are seen, most are too self-absorbed and fearful, unwilling or unable to speak of that which now is inevitably approaching. Parents today raise their children to the ethic and abstract standard of a dying world order that has no direction or future. Burdening and parasitising them, they have placed a heavy yoke upon their shoulders.

Many today are awakening to an understanding of their own participation in this hierarchy of lies and deceit. The forces of duality/darkness seek now to create greater confusion and engender chaos. Having led ignorant humanity into the arms of death, they seek humanities co-operation for their final solution and involutional harvest.

Perhaps it will be under the premise of peace, security

and promises of a new and greater world that they shall keep humanity inspired to serve and complete their true agenda?

Few truly see how the new world order has needed the participation of an ignorant people as the dark masters have set about to deceive humanity, who, in their great self-absorption are adopted and hired in their blindness! It has always been the brothers of shadow's finest play to manipulate and channel fear under the pretence of what is known as 'love' to guide and seduce humanity to achieve their greatest lie. This 'new world order' is their final hour of desperation and onslaught before they end.

And it has ever been the brothers of darkness who have always tried to install a global dictatorship under a lucerferian theocracy, though, today it is seen as an inevitable consequence and passing phase reality through which humanity must now be collectively initiated.

The so-called New Age is being seen mostly for what it is. Beguiled into illusion and sorcery, mostly its adherents are lost in spiritual egotism and materialism.

The false and limpid rise of gross humanitarian and ecological values today is but an excuse for the many who would not truly give up anything and is but a cover to hide their easily discernible apathy!

The marriage of politics and wayward religion is seen to be the dooming call of the day. Truly pitiful are the blind and corrupted priesthoods who dare pronounce their absurd dogmas and fallen perspectives in the face of their own exposure!

Religious fanaticism and aberrant occultism is growing in line with what seems to be a scripted apocalyptic vision of war and glory. This is the call of blood sacrifice, avenge and revenge, the final yet inevitable call of a dying world ego.

Despite the best of intentions, gross materialism as a way of life ends in a culture of brute violence under self-preservation. These mechanical impulses born from the fallen nature are the result of a collective humanity writhing in its own anguish and decay. The result of a world that has rejected truth and a people lost in the inertia of a wayward civilization.

Such is the day's great confusion and chaos, managed and governed by an elite hierarchy!

Great deception is at hand!

Tell us humanity, would you fight to keep this decaying corpse of a civilization animated?

Would you war to preserve your great illusions?

What lies will you tell yourselves to satisfy the greater denial, and what will you permit to satisfy your lies?

This hell that you have awakened has been born of your apathy and indifference. Surrendering your soul to the outer and the false you allow yourselves to be manipulated.

Know that those who now control you have little or no mercy for humanity and the very thin illusion of outward civility shall and cannot last for much longer, and verily, today, the writing is on the wall!

Today, many shall ask, what of those visions and promises expounded by those prophets, saints and avatars of redemption, salvation and coming glory?

It has ever been the great arrogance, folly and futility, that humanity expects divinity to contort and comply with humanity's own twisted expectations.

Individually and collectively, mankind's resulting interpretive obscuring and delusions end in disaster and madness as these end times are highlighting!

Divinity, through the forms of its servers and avatars, has always assisted wayward humanity, remaining the vital link in the great chain, though, forced to work in the background for millennia. They have been mostly maltreated, feared and scorned throughout the ages and yet their love knows no bounds.

The hierarchy of Christ fulfils its ancient pledge even today amidst the growing chaos and confusion and remains with its hand ever extended till the very end. Those who must now awaken amidst the great and growing madness are called to release their mundane and worldly attachments. This piece is not written to promote fear or false rebellion. It is, over time, to realise the illusory situation in terms of egotistic salvation or physical survival. It is time for those who can see, to understand that death is approaching and to look beyond the temporal and see the glamour and deceptions of so-called new-age spirituality.

The Beast

When we look out to the world today we see a thriving civilization, an admixed and tangled network of pulsating ideals, laws and codes maintaining its own survival and upholding its social infrastructure. Yet for many now, the world's deterioration on many levels besides the more mundane social, economic and environmental regression is becoming very apparent.

Should we look a little deeper, behind civilization's face and seemingly glossy surface reality, then perhaps those who are brave enough to take a peak will see something more sinister. In ignorance of the power and potentialities of its own creations, humanity, over countless generations and through its misunderstandings and negligence of energy and thought, have become their own victims. Through misuse of its free will, humanity has spawned a gross, energetic and semi-intelligent entity within its subtle planes. A great beast of monstrous proportions has fused its unholy aeonic and miscreant energies and taken up a life quality of its own. Plundering the minds and hearts of its victims it has taken reign and consumes those very beings that have birthed it.

We can see that humanity has lost control and is firmly under the spell of its own creation, this writhing eggragore of twisted energies that subsists off certain life forces generated by humanity.

Its servants and slaves are mostly blind automatons. Dispossessed of their soul qualities, absorbed and grafted in which their little mundane and menial lives have become but the dying batteries to sustain its very existence. Its keepers, are those possessed with its unholy intelligence and adaptable cleverness, perpetuating and maintaining its existence as they work with needle and thread to keep the very rotten and tearing fabric of this unholy civilization from falling apart completely. That they have a mind is confusing, because they think it is their own and little do they understand that it is not they who are so much living their lives but something else that is living through them.

Many people have come to the realisation that there can be occult possession of individual human microcosms but too few take notice or heed that whole worlds and civilizations can become possessed as well.

As we look at society today we see a great mass and sufferable horde of beings under the foul sway of a vast network of schooling, political and religious systems, hiding behind a thin veneer of admixed cultural expression and illusionary motivations with all but one disguised determination – to perpetuate this beast's unholy existence.

Should we review society's laws, schooling and belief structures they are but impressions and indoctrinations, imprinting the weak and the vulnerable. We hear ideals and ways of living, such as consumerism, capitalism and materialism used and accepted by the mass of humanity daily. Yet with but a little rationalisation and effort such concepts are found uniquely insane and disturbing as developed by the world as a way to sustain itself.

Our adopted religions have become just as insane. Rising fundamentalists, extremist doctrines with thoroughly confused and ignorant new age applications, all adhering to an obtuse and twisted fabric of idealisms that only compete and clash with one another with their followers' attempted application and explanation of the one true life!

Yes, if people could only see with their hearts and take an honest look at what they are becoming then they would understand what they are being drawn into and inwardly withdraw, instead of pulling each other into the beast's hungry mouth.

This beast shows no mercy for humanity's children. Their vulnerable and impressionable minds are easy targets as it indoctrinates them and infuses their hearts. Their very parents and social peers induct them into their collective madness as the beast takes them and estranges them from any inner remembrance of true life so that they know no other purpose than its own.

There are a growing number who are awakening today and are gazing into this world in horror and disgust at what it has become.

And though we ourselves in writing this piece have brought your attention to this, it is perhaps wise to emphasize that focusing one's attention upon the darkness of this world only feeds its existence. For there are imminent dangers in defining and giving this unholy creation of humanity attributes and form. This only serves to further estrange it from ourselves, lest we give it greater power and substance than it has already taken.

Many in despair may ask, how do we fight such a creature that plunders our very mind and hearts, whose eyes stare ravenously through our own eyes and whose roar is ushered from our very mouths?

Here we must say that to war with it personally or collectively is only to war upon our very selves, which is futile. This only estranges us further from that which is real and further disassociates aspects of the collective, enhancing humanity's illusions of separateness and increasing its collective madness.

Yet there is an answer and for that we must turn within. In this time of earthly madness and despair there is a call of divine Love that is awakening in the hearts of many, inspiring those whose hearts are open to seek new life as a whisper of true hope and salvation. Those who are hearing its divine cadences are turning away from this world and are becoming seekers of divine reality. These seekers of Truth are beginning to see clearly the great mess and horror of what their little lives have truly become and realise that their personal efforts to save this dying world is the very source of its misery and unholy perpetuation. They are starting to know there is a power that is greater than their selves and in this lies their only true means of truly saving themselves. It is the field of Divine Love, for only within its protective radiance are they truly safe from the evil and madness of this world. Only under its light are we given the illumination and sight to see through the darkness that has engulfed this world and thereby offer a true service to humanity.

For only its power can vanquish the miscreant forms and evil that humanity has created over successive generations.

Today there is a rallying call to all those true souls who hear the voice of Christ within their hearts to enter this field to prepare for the great influx of Divine Light and Love that shall very soon enter this world and destroy this great evil of the ages.

Beware of Feeding Drama

Those who truly understand what is transpiring today receive that which is entering this world in silence and solemnity. Verily, the breaking light of the dawn preceding the greater coming glory is being sensed and inwardly perceived by those with eyes to see and is being responded to accordingly.

Within and in spite of the deteriorating worldly conditions, Truth is entering the hearts of those who by grace and true preparedness are emptying and allowing the dissolution of self. They now await that which has inevitably been set in motion.

Sadly, for the unprepared and those who would deny that which is happening, the incoming light is forcing a bewildered world ego to scramble frantically as it struggles to comprehend and grasp that which it cannot. As collapsing structures multiply, externally as well as internally, and the world as we know it disintegrates before our eyes, those who are unable to receive the new life vibrations will only perceive the hell of a world that is drastically 'going wrong'. This is because so many are so deeply entrenched in self and duality that they are unable to still and look up to see what is truly happening.

Understand it is the entrance of New Life into this darkened world that is 'going wrong' upon this Earth; and unfortunately this world is now to bear very hard and fast lessons for its ignorance and denial.

Today there are many dangers for servers within the fast dissolution of reality as we know it. Teachings that once served us in the relative and not so distant past are falling away into the shadows of redundancy and a purely mental approach is not sufficient to receive the oncoming waves. Such people will find those solid footholds and bedrocks of truth that they might have grasped onto are crumbling, and those ideals that they have used as crutches to walk through this harsh and complicated world are coming apart. In such times it is easy to fall into confusion and moments of panic, to be drawn deeper into self or into the growing dramas and traumas of the hour.

As personalities react and the tempo is raised, madness is growing in the eyes of those so identified with the illusion. As people try to seek meaning in the meaningless or try to give substance to that which is fast dissolving, they are merely throwing fuel upon their own funeral pyres. In a play for energy, people are increasingly coerced into drama, confrontation and selfish activity. The fallen and starving matrix of human life grows desperate as light enters its realm and it realises its own inevitable demise.

Many servers have been attacked, wounded, scorned and humiliated…such are the conditions here upon this planet. In what has aptly been termed the 'Madness of end times' by some, attacks to stop, delay or end the work that aids liberation will continue until the very end. The evils of the world are seeping to the surface and Agent Smith hasn't given up. There are so many unwitting and complicit pawns to act as pretenders…seven billion souls to choose from, all of whom believe that which they are not.

In desperation those people who cling to the old world reality are becoming ever more erratic and unpredictable. Unable to stay the rising confusion and despair growing from within, many people are going insane within the growing tension.

This is also true for those who identify as humanity's benefactors. People calling themselves light-workers, star seeds and divine warriors etc., who by attaching to their idealisms and pushing their personal agendas are finding that in the light of the new day they are now being left behind very confused and somewhat speechless. The speed at which events and realisation are happening seem now to be leaving behind their foolish utterances and limp ideologies as Truth comes forth with such a momentum that their little egos cannot control or meet it.

Such people who identify themselves as their works are only clinging to self!

For those who run within today's 'spiritual circuit', how many times does one hear the same worn out platitudes and revelations of people constantly telling others about their great and grand personal missions of healing, exposing the demons, gathering the light workers together etc!

Such utterances might have served a purpose in the not so distant past but now are becoming strange and curious echoes from a reality now fading from the hearts and minds of those coming to the truest of ends.

As soon as one hears a personality step in with his or her declarations and convictions it is then the simple truth may remind us of the impotency of self and its ways…

Open your eyes and look around!

Those who are able to receive *are* being healed, the demons *are* being exposed, the true viable sparks *are* being gathered upon the inner planes – this is independent of the little roles we might play in this unfolding drama and in the growing light of that which comes, and all that is hidden shall soon clearly be revealed.

In regards to one's personality…everything in this world is subject to change. In true divine contact we remember that whatever station or assignment we might identify with or hold ourselves to is but ephemeral, temporal and impermanent, especially in these swiftly changing realities of today. Whoever has had such contact knows the foolishness of such things!

For the living and healing waters of Love Divine to cleanse our wound and resolve our pain it is necessary for us to be still and empty. In this time we are being asked to be very aware where we place our energy. It is important to give ourselves completely to God and truly distinguish that which we are *not* in this fallen and harsh reality rather than try to cling to and reinforce who we think we are…which in the face of what now comes means extremely little!

For Those Intrepid Warriors Of Love

With the intensification of global processes, we are seeing the rising effects of the planetary catharsis before our eyes in the great maelstrom of confused and deceptive reactions within the world ego at this time. The advent of certain energies into the planet are now truly making their impact felt and the old world consciousness thrashes in response.

Those who are attached or deeply identified with the maya of the world will only be consumed in its growing madness. What is needed is right response and alignment to incoming energies and not reactions to rising outward turbulence and troubles. Everywhere lies and deceit are broadcast and it is imperative that one is able to turn within and discern the inner divine truth over this play of shadows. This will be no easy feat as the madness is growing in a continual intensification.

What is needed is a deep understanding of the true art of divine surrender.

If people want to be of true assistance to the race they have to turn deep within and transcend this social matrix and its mere superficial levels of spiritual inclination. Many are unwilling and unable, and for the most part bewildered humanity is still self-centred, dangerous and very unpredictable.

The condition of the human collective is very misaligned, and its identification with the world ego means that all true spiritual work is most often hampered, confused and even opposed. True servers of the race should not expect anything different from a people who are materialistically inclined and self-centred, despite the many utterances of love and light from 'new age and spiritual circles'. Unfortunately, in this world's current climate if you are not mostly being hated or vilified you are not doing the real work!

Many people might think these are hard words but experience will reveal they are not!

It has been through grace and good fortune that over decades I have synchronistically connected with quite a few selfless, hardworking and brave servers of the race. They know who they are and their work and being bears their mark and resonance. The vibratory quality of their work and being far surpasses those who like to make an outward show of things.

It is for these beings I have written this piece.

I am not appealing or speaking to those vain and self-deluded beings that put on superficial shows of love and service. It is often those mystically deluded and self-inclined fools who are the cause of so much of the trouble to those who are aligned with the true divine work.

Over and over, some of us have watched true servers of the race be attacked, laughed at and scorned. Over many years, one here has seen great beings offer themselves in loving truth and sacrifice to a population unable to truly comprehend or care.

Knowing these are the conditions here on Earth today, true servers understand and accept that!

But also know it is often the so-called 'awakened' or new age communities that I have seen, that cause them more grief and pain than any other. Premature understandings and self-relativity often have them opposing the true servers of the race while uttering self-affirming platitudes to each other of love and light.

There are many armchair 'truthers' that like to spew their opinions and poison everywhere. Know that awakening to outer planetary manipulations or reacting to energies facilitating mere wake-up calls is still very far from consciously entering the stream of rhythmic revelation and selfless service to the underlying divine plan. This is an unfolding recognition and sustained alignment to the one living reality within. If you do not understand these words then you are still very far from the causative realities underlying your present state of being.

What is needed is silence, emptiness and going within to reach a much deeper point of discernment!

Many divine servers have to hold an alignment and resonance far beyond the self-feeding and 'high spirited' intellects and glamours of a confused and self-centred humanity. The necessity of their incarnations have come about through cosmic need and people would do well to contemplate such things instead of attacking the very messengers that are here to assist them.

Earth service is not about being loved or admired. Despite what many people assume it is not about becoming enlightened, happy, or creating a better world. Servers sacrifice all their own self desires, glamours and relativities to serve the unfolding living revelation of the divine impulse. For the most part it's about stepping out of the way so the Divine Will can enter into a world that hisses at its presence.

Often serving as energetic transmitters, the reflective and vibratory quality of a true server's presence brings up in people and communities around them things they do not wish to recognise. This leads people in their foolishness and blindness to attack servers in their misunderstandings. The higher vibratory resonance and impersonal auras of divine servers often have people attack them due to their reflective quality. Understand that we are present in a world that for the most part is anti-Christ (anti the world soul) and should be viewed as a somewhat hostile territory! (If this is not so, look how most avatars and divine personages have been treated throughout history.)

Today, the stimulating qualities of new planetary energies are also stimulating certain 'seeds of evil' that lay in people's microcosms. Things are ramping up! This is happening both at an individual and collective level as past karma and egomaniacal realities are brought to the surface. Those with false offerings to spirit are today unable to hold their outward show and pose of 'goodness'.

True servers are mostly hated and vilified through their short sojourn upon this fallen earth but they are never left bereft of Love, power and true guidance. Part of the transmutation process has them turn such pain and hatred into beautiful gems that shall adorn their crown of earth service. For the adept of the race, these times offer unprecedented grace, and favour one's ability to deeply surrender to the incoming light and energies that offer true and powerful protection.

Today, there are those who stand within the collective that are receiving more powerful energies and subtle guidance that bring with them the appropriate divine intelligence and protection to handle the rising darkness and confusion.

Verily the dawn breaks... As one here looks out over the swelling and tumultuous sea and observes those intrepid and beautiful souls who stand as veritable islands of light in this mad and crazy world, only respect and gratitude fill this heart.

May our Great Father God bless you all!

The Fire of God's Love

Everyone knows how they are living is wrong...

Selfishness, materialism, egotism thrive in our so-called modern culture. We parasite off Mother Earth with no care to the damage we are doing! Everyone uses and abuses each other to keep themselves afloat. We subject our children to a miscreant society that enslaves their minds and poisons their hearts.

Our civilization is sick, we are sick and the symptoms go unheeded. We see the desecration of the sacred in almost everything we do. Our lives oblivious to the call to change.

Did you think this would be allowed to continue!

Powerful energies are now being released through our Earth. Today the Divine Spirit comes into manifestation and with it comes the burning of all that will not receive it.

Judgement is here!

One here does not speak of the blinded and fiery zeal of the misguided church evangelists and their congregations who shout condemnation, the foolishness of new age thought or the projections of the so-called truth movement.

Despite the disbelief or the sarcasms of the unheeding or spiritually dead, the great change has now come and is still coming. Everyone will pass through these fires.

Divine imposition is an act of God's mercy. The flaming sword of Truth is being driven through to the core of our beings. The avatar comes when we are unwilling or incapable of changing, when we are pulling ourselves and each other into hell!

Now it is change or be changed!

People's worlds are falling apart. Their cherished belief systems and the lies that they tell themselves are being revealed for what they are. Many are having past events in their lives resurface in their minds, most are feeling an unknown pressure, others are contracting in fear. Karmic processes are coming back at a remarkable pace. All are symptoms of these cosmic fires entering our Earth.

People are looking for others to blame. They cling to the religions, intellectualisms, sciences to evade the Truth. The fearful will try to scuttle like cockroaches under their rocks but all is in vain for their safe houses will be overturned. Their hiding places and darkness revealed in the light that bores its way downwards into the hearts of all of humankind.

You cannot stop what has come into this world...but you can embrace it!

The energies that are growing in intensity are the

fires of God's Love. With them comes our redemption.

The pure in heart shall greet Truth's fire. Let it bring to the surface all the filth, rubbish and stupidity we have lived in these foolish little lives. In the cosmic fire lies regeneration, our transformation and with it comes the presence of God. For those who understand, 'God's Wrath' contains the sweetest Love and realisation.

It is time to let it all go. This way of life that creates deep suffering, the pain of an existence with no hope but spiritual death. The new is here!

The Divine Fire will keep growing in intensity, until we fall to our knees. Everything impure will burn and continue to burn. The horror of civilization stands revealed! It shall now fall. Let us all fall to our knees.

For those with eyes to see, the remarkable is now being revealed, God is showing his hand. The great tempering is now. Soon, no one will be able to deny! Soon everyone will see the truth face to face and know where they stand.

God be praised! The great Change is here!

A Child of Universal Love

We have been on guard throughout this earth sojourn, unable to trust in these shadows that parade before us. The cries of pain and torture, the wails of torment like a hurricane whirl around us in the injustices of this world.

We have been badly damaged; we damage each other just by being in proximity.

The noise and pollution of modern civilization…

We use and abuse each other to keep ourselves afloat.

Devils stare at us through the eyes of those around us. We recoil, pretending we do not see...but we do!

No one to trust, no one is truly our friend, each with their own selfish agenda, each in their own pain. Even our earth parents are so damaged through their ancestry, their misaligned realities and the afflictions of life, they are unable to do anything but stumble blindly around often doing us more damage than good.

A child's life unfolds so delicately. Who remembers the fragile longing of a young girl in expectation of her father coming home, the embrace of the young boy in the breast of his mother? Every moment with our children is a gift but in the cold reality that is the world, who meets them in that moment?

On Earth we have forgotten so much.

Today, Life is calling...the longing of a pure Love that sings as a gentle song in our hearts.

Upon the ethers I often hear the sweetest voice...

It says, "Come home!"

It is a remembrance of Universal Love...the whispers of the Divine Parent.

In prayer, a yearning takes my being, raising my heart…as waves of ethereal love flood down from above. I shut my eyes absorbed in this soft gentle bliss. These end days have become moments opened to an eternal window...within this fading dream of earth life.

My innermost heart opens, gently surging and pulsing. I proceed in caution. It has been so long since I have been able to trust in a world bereft of sincerity. Images quickly flicker through my mind's eye as fading earth dreams, with flashes of my childhood. I recall each time I tried to share God's Love and how it was rejected. An unknown but familiar voice sings to me, the remembrance floods through...I let go into the continuum of light with the instinct of a child running into his mother's arms. It all washes away in a surge of warmth and my eyes open. In the realm of the golden central sun I awaken as a newborn child.

The kiss of a new life beckons from the Universal Mother's lips and she smiles. She is my very breath and my newly formed heart bubbles with joy. Unfolding, stretching in my Father's great cosmic palm, looking into a sea of eternal Love.

"We have you now," she whispers into my mind, as waves of bliss wash my newly opened eyes.

Absorbed in the Father's warm embrace, the purity of my Mother resonates in my heart. I raise my fingers into the vast spectrum of pure light. The knowing and assurance of the Divine Parent strengthens my spirit in absolute trust. Having been birthed into infinity…

Today, as this earth disappears from my sight, my whisper to all earth parents… remember your children! They are not yours. You are but custodians for our Father/Mother God and what you do today in this time of change shall be heard in the highest courts!

Give them a chance, let go of your fears, let them breathe and they will reveal to you what you have long since forgotten.

The sacredness of life can be seen in a child's eyes. Their heartbeat is the heartbeat of God…

Let them fly; theirs is a destiny far different from yours.

A New World begins...

www.ingramcontent.com/pod-product-compliance
Lightning Source LLC
Chambersburg PA
CBHW021129300426
44113CB00006B/356